"This book is a Bible study, a personal trek rather than the diary of someone else's journey. Each chapter has three parts: (1) a concise, well-written introduction to a woman described in the Bible; (2) a collection of related Bible texts that take a deep dive into this woman's real, personal decisions; and (3) a toolbox of questions to weigh her choices against the most important teachings of the Bible."
—Glenn Parkinson, Pastor Emeritus, Severna Park Evangelical Presbyterian Church

"It is a pleasure to endorse this series of Bible studies on thirty-two women of the Bible. May God's blessing be on each one who picks up the Bible and is led by the series of questions to ask themselves very similar questions so that we all may grow up in Christ Jesus. Special thanks to Joanne Guarnieri Hagemeyer for a beautiful piece of work."
—Walt Kaiser, former President of Gordon-Conwell Theological Seminary

"This is an excellent book of studies on biblical female figures, some of whom are relatively obscure. Joanne Guarnieri Hagemeyer has provided helpful contextual introductory notes for each woman being studied, and a series of probing questions encourage the reader to wrestle with and apply the biblical material. I would commend it to any reader looking for a topical study on the women of the Bible."
—Joanna Barlow, psychiatrist, Teaching Leader, and sought-after consultant on women's issues in the Australian Presbyterian Church

"By combining illuminating historical backgrounds, comprehensive Scripture readings, and profound questions, these studies situate you in the cultural and emotional contexts of thirty-two biblical women."
—Denise Murphy Plichta, author of *Redemptive History and Theology*

"Many studies on women in the Bible have been written in our modern time. Yet in *Broken, Searching, Trusted, Powerful*, Joanne has been able to provide a fresh and thorough survey on the topic, along with valuable questions to reflect upon. For anyone wanting to dive into further exploration of God's work amongst women in Scripture, I commend her study to you."
—Scott Lencke, author of *Change for the First Time, Again* and *Reflections of Immanuel*

"Searching for an in-depth Bible study that will move you past the superficial into deep biblical truth? Look no further. This book will draw you into the lives of thirty-two women in Scripture whose experiences will foster a fresh understanding of a powerful and loving God. Study questions will encourage thoughtful responses and meaningful application for any student of God's word. I highly recommend this book for personal or group study."
—Julie Zine Coleman, Bible teacher and author of *Unexpected Love: God's Heart Revealed through Jesus' Conversations with Women*

BROKEN, SEARCHING, TRUSTED, POWERFUL

BROKEN, SEARCHING, TRUSTED, POWERFUL

Thirty-two Biblical Women Whose Impact is Still Felt Today

J. GUARNIERI HAGEMEYER

RESOURCE Publications • Eugene, Oregon

BROKEN, SEARCHING, TRUSTED, POWERFUL
32 Biblical Women Whose Impact Is Still Felt Today

Copyright © 2020 J. Guarnieri Hagemeyer. All rights reserved. Except for brief quotations in critical publications or reviews, no part of this book may be reproduced in any manner without prior written permission from the publisher. Write: Permissions, Wipf and Stock Publishers, 199 W. 8th Ave., Suite 3, Eugene, OR 97401.

Wipf & Stock
An Imprint of Wipf and Stock Publishers
199 W. 8th Ave., Suite 3
Eugene, OR 97401

www.wipfandstock.com

PAPERBACK ISBN: 978-1-7252-7770-0
HARDCOVER ISBN: 978-1-7252-7769-4
EBOOK ISBN: 978-1-7252-7771-7

Manufactured in the U.S.A.

This book is dedicated to Anita Gutschick of Women of the Bible, LLC, who, through her powerful portrayals of biblical women, and her giftedness in spiritual insight and encouragement, empowered me where I lacked courage.

CONTENTS

FOREWORD 1
PREFACE 3
INTRODUCTION 5
BROKEN 7
    Abigail 7
    Bathsheba 11
    Wife of Lot 15
    Leah 19
THIRSTY 23
    Rebekah 23
    Woman at the Well 27
    Hagar 31
    Miriam 35
FOREIGNER 39
    Rahab 39
    Ruth 43
    Herodias 47
    Esther 51
IMPRISONED 55
    Eve 55
    Daughter of Jairus 59
    Wife of Potiphar 63

Mary of Magdala 67
TRUSTED... 71
    Puah.. 71
    Sarah... 75
    Wife of Job 79
    Martha... 83
SEARCHING 87
    Wife of Pilate... 87
    Elizabeth 91
    Wife of Noah 95
    Woman Caught in Adultery............................. 99
POWERFUL 103
    Anna.. 103
    Witch of Endor 107
    Jezebel.. 111
    Lydia.. 115
INTIMATE... 119
    Mary of Bethany... 119
    Virgin Mary 123
    Delilah 127
    Sinful Woman 131
A FINAL WORD.. 135
    Acknowledgements.. 135
    Meet the Author 137

FOREWORD

Anita Gutschick, Women of the Bible, LLC

Story can capture our imagination, evoke laughter, or bring tears. A story can give us a different point of view or expose us to something new. Story is powerful. Without doubt, the most read "story" over history has been the Bible. God's story. I view it as a love story. There is no doubt when reading it that God deeply loves his people.

As an actress, I am interested in story and the characters in the story. Through a series of events (I believe a part of God's plan), I became interested in some of the stories of the women in Scripture. At first, I was only looking at them from an actress's point of view. What is the woman's objective or obstacle? What tactics will she employ to reach her objective? The kind of questions that enliven a scene.

But as God continued to provide opportunities for me to tell some of his stories through the eyes of the women he had preserved in Scripture, I began to recognize the sacredness of these stories. Furthermore, I realized just how much God loved women, even in the patriarchal society that existed during Biblical times. Since 1995, I have had the honor of portraying many of the Biblical women and watch God move in the hearts of women and men as they hear and feel these stories. God's stories speak to us today.

Not long after answering God's call to devote myself full-time to the telling of his sacred stories, I went to a Bible Study Fellowship women's group. Frankly, I went hoping to let the organizers know about my work. I thought, surely they had conferences or events and could use my services.

However, it became painfully clear early on, that God had me there not for marketing, but because I needed to be closer in touch with him.

Through that experience I had the privilege of sitting under the teaching of Joanne. She blew me away. Even when I would crawl into class after having a tough week of traveling and portrayals, I was always invigorated by her vibrant teaching. Her love and reverence for Scripture was infectious. Never in my wildest dream did I envision us collaborating. But God can knit people together, and he certainly did that for us. But make no mistake, this lovely book, "Heroine or Villainess?" is completely the excellent work of Joanne.

From the beginning of my adventure with these Biblical women, God has placed three things on my heart:

- God is in the business of using ordinary and sometimes broken people.
- God preserved the stories of many women, some of which remain unnamed.
- These women are reaching across the generations to encourage and empower us.

It is my firm believe that in walking through this study, that Joanne has so thoughtfully and lovingly prepared, you too will be encouraged and perhaps empowered by the lives of these women who lived so long ago. Even though their circumstances may have looked far different from our lives today, the condition of the heart has not changed. Enjoy their stories from the past that bring lessons for today and hope for tomorrow.

PREFACE

Welcome

The following Bible studies have been crafted to engage both your intellect and your imagination, your reasoning powers and your emotional acumen, your "left" brain and your "right" brain. Each study is designed to help you see for yourself what the passage says, what it means, and how God is involving you.

It is my hope for you to experience something fresh and new from the pages of this ancient, yet living, document—God's Word—as well as to experience the enrichment of spiritual and emotional connection, as you engage in each part of the study.

In order to provide enough time to experience the study material, to absorb the information and process it, please consider meeting in a group setting for about an hour each week to talk about what you have discovered and learned, to process how the Bible story affects you, and how you sense God is working through the study in your inner life.

Please give yourself plenty of time to think, pray, and study in between meetings. Consider journaling during your experience, as so often the Lord provides insights when you are willing to spend time listening to his voice within you, after you have studied, prayed, talked, read, and pondered.

Please take risks in this study. Talk with each other about your life, about what you feel, or see, or think of, and how God is working this material into your spirit. Picture yourself inside the story, looking all around at the world this ancient woman lived in. Ask questions. Listen well to each other, think mindfully about each other's questions and thoughts, for this is the Spirit of Christ speaking among you.

If you feel new to Bible study or to prayer, Ancient Voices, Sacred Stories offers a free introduction to both, on Udemy:

Introduction to Prayer:

https://www.udemy.com/ancient-voices-sacred-stories-introduction-to-prayer/learn/v4/overview

Introduction to the Bible:

https://www.udemy.com/ancient-voices-sacred-stories-introduction-to-the-bible/learn/v4/overview

As you go through the reading assignments and the accompanying questions, do what you can as the Lord leads. Take the time you need to share about how God is changing you as you take his words to heart.

For more information about online courses and weekend retreats, please visit:

www.AncientVoicesSacredStories.com

or

www.GraceAndPeaceJoanne.com

Grace and peace to you, Joanne

"To him who is able to keep you from stumbling and to present you before his glorious presence without fault and with great joy—to the only God our Savior be glory, majesty, power and authority, through Jesus Christ our Lord, before all ages, now and forevermore!" (Jude 24–25)

Unless otherwise noted, all Scripture references are taken from THE HOLY BIBLE, NEW INTERNATIONAL VERSION®, NIV® Copyright © 1973, 1978, 1984, 2011 by Biblica, Inc.™ Used by permission. All rights reserved worldwide.

INTRODUCTION

About This Study

At first glance, it may seem as though the Bible is populated mostly with the stories of faithful men, courageous men, or nefarious men—men who were either enemies or friends of God. Mostly stories of men.

Added to the difficulty of seeing women in the pages of Scripture is the effort it takes to "hear" their voices and understand their stories. The sixty-six books of the Bible itself were written largely from the male point of view, concentrating on male heroes and villains. (Only the books of Ruth and Esther focus on a woman, and neither one is written from an explicitly female lens.) Women most often become—at best—supporting characters. Without thinking about it, we've accepted this point of view and this unspoken role for women across time. We've accepted looking at women through men's eyes.

But a second glance reveals the stories of often-unnamed women as living faithfully and courageously for God, as well as some living powerfully and villainously against God. Regardless of whose point of view is reflected in the stories we read in Scripture, women, as much as men, have contributed to the great narrative of God and humanity.

Remaining unnamed does not mean remaining without impact or legacy. All of the women in this book have left a lasting mark on history. Their stories are in the Scriptures to encourage and exhort us as God writes his story into our own lives. For as much as women and men have for centuries gained insight, spiritual growth, and encouragement in their lives of faith through the men portrayed in the Bible, so also we can gain the same bracing illumination through women's accounts which God himself inspired these ancient writers of Scripture to record. May their grit and tenacity, their dignity and tragedy embolden you and me to live out our faith to the full.

In the words of the apostle Paul, may it be that according to the riches of God's glory, God grant that we may be strengthened in our inner beings with power through God's Spirit, and that the Lord Jesus may dwell in our hearts through faith, as you and I are being rooted and grounded in love, receiving instruction through the word of the Lord (Ephesians 3:16–17).

BROKEN

Abigail

1 Samuel 25; 1 Samuel 27:3; 1 Samuel 30:3, 5, 18; 2 Samuel 2:2; 3:3; 1 Chronicles 2:16–17; 3:1

Abigail was married to Nabal, one of the wealthiest men in the region. He owned enormous herds and a great many acres of land in Carmel, a province of Judah, west of the Dead Sea. Since marriages at this time represented alliances and economic covenants, Abigail undoubtedly also came from a wealthy and landed family within the tribe of Judah. Her dowry, along with her family's prestige and influence, would have enhanced Nabal's inheritance, just as his affluence would have secured her future.

Nabal was a descendant of the famous Caleb who, along with Joshua, had led all Israel to conquer Canaan. Caleb, one of the twelve spies, and Joshua, Moses' right-hand man, were the only two people of all those who had come through the wilderness to be granted by God the privilege of entering the Promised Land.

Interestingly, Caleb had been a Kenizzite, a descendant of one of the indigenous people groups already living in Canaan. Tantalizing clues found in such passages as Exodus 12:38, which states a "mixed crowd also went up with them," reveal an intriguing detail of the exodus. It seems other, non-Hebrew people such as Egyptians, and undoubtedly other enslaved peoples such as, possibly, the Kenizzites, joined forces and faith with God and his people.

Caleb was given Hebron as his inheritance from the Lord, within the tribe of Judah. These rich, rolling hills in Nabal's holdings were Caleb's legacy.

But Nabal seems not to have inherited the mettle and good character of his renowned ancestor. The Bible describes him as surly and mean, a man given to drunkenness, ingratitude, miserliness, rudeness, and disrespect. One can only guess what being married to him must have been like for Abigail.

On the other hand, God makes a point of highlighting Abigail's intelligence as well as her beauty. She was trusted by the servants who accepted her authority with high regard. She was good at organizing, was quick thinking, swift to action, and able to provide. Abigail was also humble and honoring to others. When she spoke, she was bold, direct, wise, and spiritually mature. Abigail was well known for her gracious hospitality, providing abundantly for her guests during the traditionally joyful sheep-shearing festival.

How could a marriage so broken, weighted by the burden of abuse and unchecked addiction, bring any good to Abigail? And yet, God had a magnificent purpose in this apparently mismatched couple, as Abigail's story reveals.

Read 1 Samuel 25 and Proverbs 31:10–31
1. Compare Abigail with the wife described in Proverbs.

2. Contrast the conversation between Nabal and David's men with Abigail and the servants.

Read Leviticus 25:35 and Deuteronomy 15:7–11
3. Describe Nabal's words and actions towards David and his men, in light of God's word.

4. Describe Abigail's words and actions towards David and his men, in light of God's word.

5. What did God say would happen as a result of how one responds to his command (Deuteronomy 15:7–11)?

6. How did God's word prove true in Nabal's life? In Abigail's life?

Read Matthew 25:34–36 and Luke 12:41–43
7. Consider what the Lord Jesus says on this same topic to believers today. How faithful are you with the resources you have been blessed with?

Read 1 Samuel 25; 1 Samuel 27:2–3; 2 Samuel 7:11b–16; 2 Samuel 23:1–7; and Matthew 1:1–17
8. Describe Abigail's appeal to David.

How did Abigail protect her husband? Who did she say was at fault?

How did she honor David?

What were her requests?

9. What prophetic statement did Abigail make? How was it fulfilled?

10. What do you do and say when you are faced with conflict? How does God's word inform your words and actions?

11. In what ways did David respond to each statement and request?

12. What lessons and truths have you learned from studying Abigail's story?

13. What does this passage reveal about God?

14. How is your character and spiritual life challenged by Abigail's story?

15. In what ways will you live out what God is teaching you? Be specific.

BROKEN

Bathsheba

2 Samuel 11; 12:10–24; 1 Kings 1:11–31; 2:13–19; 1 Chronicles 3:5; Psalm 51:1; Matthew 1:6

Bathsheba was a lovely young woman, the daughter of one of King David's "Mighty Men," Eliam. Her grandfather was Ahithophel, one of David's most trusted advisors: Scripture states his wisdom was like that of someone who always inquired of God. Bathsheba, as was the custom of her day, had married at a young age to another of David's close friends and member of his royal guard, Uriah the Hittite, whose name indicates he had either converted to Judaism, or had at least shown great loyalty to David and to Israel.

Uriah's name derives from the Hittite Empire, which had reached its zenith six hundred years earlier, then collapsed due to a series of devastating wars. By David's time, the Hittite empire had been reduced to several city-states, which in turn were all either conquered or annexed by the time of Bathsheba's grandson's reign. It is possible Uriah was a wandering mercenary who had joined David in the early years when he was fleeing Saul. Uriah was eventually recognized as one of the king's thirty-seven (later expanding to about eighty) best warriors, memorialized as the "Mighty Men."

Jewish law required newly married men to stay home for a year. As the Bible demurely puts it, "If a man has recently married, he must not be sent to war or have any other duty laid on him. For one year he is to be free to stay at home and bring happiness to the wife he has married." (Deuteronomy 24:5) For a while Uriah was able to enjoy his beautiful bride, Bathsheba. But when spring came . . .

King David was, by now, about fifty years old. He had been king of all Israel for a few years, and had finally finished his last big, multi-nation war campaign. Maybe David concluded that he had worked hard, fought the good fight, and it was time for a king to have a little rest, a little kickback time. Ever feel like that? So, when other kings were going off to war, David sent his army—including Uriah—with General Joab, while he stayed home. It was the first of many poor decisions which ultimately ended in death for Uriah, death for Bathsheba's first child, and the death of David's dream to build God's temple. Bathsheba endured what was most likely the horror of rape, the shame of an ill-gotten pregnancy, the tragic loss of her husband and baby, and the humiliation of becoming yet another addition to a rich man's harem. Bathsheba's life seemed irreparably broken.

How could God bring any good out of such suffering? How could a marriage begun so poorly hold any promise? Yet the lowest degradation led to the highest honor in Bathsheba's story.

Read 2 Samuel 11, 12:1–9 and chapters 13–18
1. How did King David come to notice Bathsheba? Explain whether you think she meant to get his attention.

2. According to Leviticus 15:19–30, what is the significance of the parenthetical statement in 2 Samuel 11:4?

12 *Heroine or Villainess?*

3. Was there any chance Bathsheba was already pregnant when David took her? Explain your answer.

4. According to Leviticus 20:10 and Deuteronomy 22:22, what penalty did both David and Bathsheba face?

5. Who actually paid that penalty, and how? (see 2 Samuel 11:24; 12:13–18)

   How was Bathsheba affected?

6. How have you been affected when you have gone against God's ways?

   What comfort have you found?

Read 1 Kings 1:11–31; 2:13–19; 1 Chronicles 3:5 and Matthew 1:6
7. Who were Bathsheba's children?

   Which child became famous, and why?

8. Describe Bathsheba's position and influence in King David's court.

9. According to these passages, which two important people approached Bathsheba for counsel, or a favor?

   What did they want, and how did she respond? How do you respond to requests for help?

10. Describe the honor Bathsheba was given by King Solomon.

11. What great spiritual honor did God bestow on Bathsheba?

12. What lessons and truths have you learned from studying Bathsheba's story?

13. What does this passage reveal about God?

14. How is your character and spiritual life challenged by Bathsheba's story?

15. In what ways will you live out what God is teaching you? Be specific.

BROKEN

Wife of Lot

---

*Genesis 13:8–13; Genesis 14; Genesis 18:16–33; Genesis 19;
Luke 17:28–33*

Lot's wife was most likely a native of Sodom, as she is first mentioned after Lot chose to settle his tents and herds among the people of the plains.
All five cities of the plain, according to thousands of cuneiform tablets discovered back in the 1970s, date to about 2,700 BC. At that time the Dead Sea had fresh water flowing into it, making the surrounding area fertile enough to sustain fields and farms, attractive enough to draw nomadic herders such as Lot and his caravan.

Lot was a man of obvious wealth, with his numerous herds, flocks and attendants. After meeting with the city elders concerning provision of fields and wells, Lot would have been invited to every affluent home to meet Sodom's eligible daughters. Handsome and prosperous, exotic and foreign, the woman who married him would have been envied by all.

It says something about Lot that he settled down, entered into a covenant of marriage and citizenship with Sodom's upper class, and built a family, a life, and a reputation among its inhabitants. Lot's wife must have loved her city, her beautiful home, her life of privilege and relative ease. Yet, Sodom's wickedness and degeneracy were legendary, so terrible that the people's cry for rescue summoned Almighty God. Still, Lot remained.

Even in the face of God's impending judgment, both Lot and his wife wavered and lingered till dawn, though they clearly understood God's warning to them. Finally, when matters became desperate, the angels who had come to deliver them had to physically pull Lot, his wife, and his daughters out of the city, crying, "Flee for your lives! Do not look back, and do not stop anywhere in the plain! Flee to the mountains or you will be swept away!" (Genesis 19:17)

Some scientists have suggested the cities of the plain were destroyed by lightning setting fire to the tar pits that had saturated the area. Concurrent earthquakes would have caused violent explosions, causing fire and brimstone to literally rain down all over the plain. Many archaeologists believe the discovery of ruins lying today under the waters of the Dead Sea are the remains of Sodom and Gomorrah and the rest of the plain cities. Very near this area is a range of hills comprised mostly of salt, in Arabic called the "Mountain of Sodom."

As Lot's wife stopped, turned, and gazed at the fire of God's wrath burning her beloved city, brimstone must have fallen on her as well. Something broke in her in that moment. She was caught by the flames and burned where she stood, before Lot's horrified eyes. Her body must have later been encrusted with the salt as the winds blew across her, becoming the pillar of verse.

It was quite a word picture the Lord Jesus would later evoke when he referred to Lot's wife in his description of the event the Jewish people had been looking forward to for thousands of years—The Great And Terrible Day of the Lord.

Read Genesis 13:8–13; Genesis 14; Genesis 18:16–33; Genesis 19
1. From the above passages, describe Sodom and the cities in the plain. (See Genesis 13:13; 14:10, 23; 19:1–5.)

2. What did Lot choose and why?

3. How might Sodom's culture have affected Lot's wife's:

Values?

Beliefs?

Spirituality?

What influence might Lot's wife have had on him?

From Genesis 18:4–5 and 18:14, describe the men Lot's daughters were pledged to marry.

4. In what ways are you and your family affected by your culture?

5. What had Abraham already done for Lot and his family? (See Genesis 14.)

   What warning might Lot and his wife have taken from this experience?

   What lessons do you learn from this story?

6. What did God tell Abraham about Sodom?

   Why was Abraham concerned?

   Provide at least two principles from this passage concerning God's judgment of the rest of the world.

7. What happened to Lot's wife and why? (See also Luke 17:32–33.)

8. What might you be continually looking back at that keeps you from living fully in the present?

Where might you feel like you are unable to go forward with your life because you feel stuck in your past?

9. What eventually happened with Lot's daughters?

10. What did Lot and his family lose by choosing to live in Sodom?

    What could Lot and his wife have done to avoid the tragic end that befell both themselves and their family?

11. Show how Genesis 19 illustrates 1 Corinthians 3:14–15 using 2 Peter 2:6–8.

12. What lessons and truths have you learned from studying the story of Lot's wife?

13. What does this passage reveal about God?

14. How is your character and spiritual life challenged by the story of Lot's wife?

15. In what ways will you live out what God is teaching you? Be specific.

BROKEN

Leah

Genesis 29; 30:9–20; 31:4–16, 33; 33:1–7; 34:1; 35:23–26;
46:8–18; 49:31; Ruth 4:11

For all her spiritual depth and desire to please, Leah seemed to face dim prospects for marriage. Yes, Leah had a gentle and tender disposition, but her sister Rachel was noticeably more beautiful, with a lively disposition. Leah was sweet, but Rachel was sizzling hot! Nevertheless, even Rachel had no serious suitors, for these sisters came from a God-fearing family, and there were not many men suitable to choose from in the surrounding population.

Their clan had traditionally worshiped other gods until God spoke to Abraham at their family homestead in Ur of the Chaldeans. After conferring with Abraham's father Terah and his brother Nahor, the whole clan decided to pull up stakes and relocate to the northern Levant in response to God's direction. Perhaps because Abraham's other brother Haran had died, leaving a young son, Lot, Terah was ready to leave his grief behind him, and start afresh in a new place. Together, the family dedicated their new settlement to Haran. When Terah died, God again spoke to Abraham, guiding him to move his tents even farther south, where he eventually settled. It seems Nahor also moved his tents and established a town in his own name.

Years later, now a wealthy patriarch, Abraham had sought a bride for his beloved son Isaac from within the extended family because of their relationship with God. Abraham did not want his son to marry into any of the local people groups with their foreign gods. Having obeyed God's command to settle in Hebron, Abraham would send his most trusted servant on a long journey north to the new family seat in Nahor (southwest of where Bethlehem would later stand). Through a series of unusual events, Rachel and Leah's aunt Rebekah—their father Laban's sister—had become Isaac's wife. Surely the miraculous story of how Rebekah had been discovered, and how her whirlwind wedding had been arranged, remained a vivid story within the whole extended family, and certainly within Laban's household.

Now, a generation later, it seems likely both Leah and Rachel, Laban's daughters, would have daydreamed about being discovered by their own future husbands. When their cousin Jacob arrived in their hometown of Paddan-Aram, Rachel and Leah must have been overjoyed! A handsome young man from their clan had come at just the right time! But the moment Jacob saw the beautiful Rachel, he fell in love with her; and before she could start, Leah was finished.

During the next seven years Leah remained unmarried, which determined the unusual events leading to her wedding day. How could God allow such an unhappy marriage of unrequited love, intense loneliness, continuing rejection, and Leah's broken heart, with seemingly no hope for change? And yet the Lord did have a plan in mind, a purpose so crucial it involved the salvation of the world: for the faith that matured in Leah was the faith her sons would grow up in.

Read Genesis 29 and 30:9–20

1. Describe Leah's wedding day, and how she came to be Jacob's bride.

2. How long did Leah have Jacob to herself? What do you think Leah did, and hoped would happen?

    What did happen when that time was up?

Heroine or Villainess?

3. What one thing did Leah want more than anything else?

   How did she go about achieving her heart's desire?

4. Compare Genesis 48:7 with Genesis 49:31 and explain whether you think Leah got her wish.

5. What would you say you long for the most? How are you trying to gain it?

   Explain why you think God will, or will not, grant your desire.

6. Find and describe the turning point in Leah's faith.

7. Where might God be leading you to turn in loving trust to him?

Read Genesis 34 and 35:23–26
8. Name Leah's children. Who were the two children attributed to Leah through her servant Zilpah?

9. Think about Dinah's experience growing up in her family, watching her parents. How do you think that affected Dinah?

What would she long for, and how would she try to find her heart's desire?

10. What were Simeon's and Levi's relationship to Dinah, and to Leah? How does that help explain their actions?

    How might your relationship(s) be affecting those you care for?

11. What spiritual honor was given to two of Israel's tribes descending from Leah's sons?

    How does that honor reflect back to Leah?

12. What lessons and truths have you learned from studying Leah's story?

13. What does this passage reveal about God?

14. How is your character and spiritual life challenged by Leah's story?

15. In what ways will you live out what God is teaching you? Be specific.

THIRSTY

Rebekah

Genesis 22:23; 24:1–66; 25:2–26:16, 34, 35;
27:5–15, 41–46; 28:5; 49:31

Rebekah, whose name meant "captivating," was the daughter of Bethuel and granddaughter of Milcah and Nahor, Abraham's brother.

A generation earlier, at God's command, Abraham and his brother Nahor, along with their father, had emigrated from Chaldea—modern-day Syria—to Haran (located in modern-day Turkey), where they stopped for a time. After their father Terah died, both Abraham and Nahor again resettled their families, journeying into Canaan, as God had originally instructed. Abraham continued south and arranged his tents near Shechem, in the hill country just below Mount Gerizim, now the West Bank of Israel. Nahor established his city in the northern Levant, among a tribal confederation of Aramaic-speaking people called Arameans.

Their clan was now associated with the Arameans, as Nahor's son Bethuel had built their family home in Aram-naharaim, near to the city of Nahor. It is possible Bethuel was quite elderly when his daughter Rebekah's story takes place, as her brother Laban seems to have acted as the head of household in her marriage negotiations. By Rebekah's selfless act of giving water to Abraham's servant and his caravan of thirsty camels, she had unknowingly revealed herself as God's intended wife for Isaac.

This account of Rebekah's ancient wedding portrays how marriages were arranged in antiquity, which included four main parts:

1. *Arrangements*, made by the fathers. Though Laban filled the central role of negotiator, the Bible is careful to report both Laban and his father Bethuel were ultimately in agreement with the final contract.

2. *A year-long betrothal*, which the bride and groom entered into if they each freely agreed to the marriage. This is what caused a certain level of consternation in Rebekah's family—the betrothal period would be spent en route to the groom's home, leaving Rebekah with no chance to even meet her betrothed.

3. *A brief wedding ceremony*. In fact, in Rebekah's story, the ceremony was reduced to a few words spoken before entering Isaac's tent.

4. *A week-long celebration*.

Theologians have long associated Rebekah's account with God's redemption of believers: Rebekah's story is embedded in the much larger metanarrative of God's relationship with Abraham, with the nation of Israel—which would count Abraham as its forefather,—and with all believers who would see Abraham as their spiritual father.

There are four main characters: Abraham, his chief servant, Isaac, and Rebekah. Abraham stands for God the Father, sending his unnamed servant into the far country to take a bride for his son, though she does not yet know she has been chosen. The servant is like the Holy Spirit, inviting her to come, to woo and win her, and bring her back to the Father's house. Isaac is like Jesus, the sacrificial lamb who is resurrected, ready to receive and claim his beloved for himself. Rebekah is seen to be like the believer who chooses to leave her old life and enter, by faith, into communion with the Lord.

Read Genesis 22:23; 24:1–66

1. What sign did the servant ask God for? Was this a reasonable sign to request?

2. Describe Rebekah's character.

3. How were Rebekah and Isaac related? (See Genesis 11:27–29; 22:20–24; 24:15, 29.)

   Why is spiritual compatibility so important? (See Deuteronomy 7:1–4; Ezra 9:11–12; 2 Corinthians 6:14-15.)

4. What evidence did Rebekah have to trust Abraham's servant?

   Why do you think Rebekah agreed to go with the servant?

5. How is Rebekah's story like a believer's union with Christ?

   Just as the servant offered Rebekah wealth, with promise of more, what wealth does the Holy Spirit offer believers? (See Acts 2:17–18; Ephesians 1:3–14, 17–21.)

   How have you experienced the Holy Spirit's treasure? How has this affected your trust in God?

Read Genesis 25:20–26:16, 34–35

6. In what ways was Isaac supportive of Rebekah, and in what ways was he not?

Supportive	Unsupportive
(Example: 25:21)	(Example: 26:7)

   How might this have affected their marriage?

7. Describe Rebekah's and Isaac's relationships with each of their sons. How might this have affected the brothers?

8. How did each son develop spiritually? Give specific examples.

   How do your family dynamics affect you spiritually? Emotionally?

Read Genesis 27:5–15, 41–46; 28:5; 49:31

9. Try to find all the layers of lies, deception, and manipulation in this story.

   What motivated Rebekah? (Compare Genesis 25:23 with Genesis 12:1–3, 7; 13:14–16; 17:4–9.)

10. Why do you think Rebekah did not trust God to keep his promise in his own way?

    What keeps you from trusting God?

11. What great sacrifice did Rebekah have to make?

    How have you been affected by your faith in God or lack of faith?

12. What lessons and truths have you learned from studying Rebekah's story?

13. What does this passage reveal about God?

14. How is your character and spiritual life challenged by Rebekah's story?

15. In what ways will you live out what God is teaching you? Be specific.

THIRSTY

Woman at the Well

John 4:3–42

All of us have two deep-seated, God-given longings. The first longing is to be truly and completely known and accepted, to be fully understood and loved. Imagine a relationship in which every emotion, every issue, is important and treated gently, with warmth and respect.

The other longing is to know that our lives are worth something, that we have meaning and purpose in the world, that who we are, and what we do, matters.

The story of the woman at the well comes right after Jesus made a blockbuster statement to the Pharisee and Sanhedrin member Nicodemus: God loves not just Pharisees, not even just Judeans, but the whole world. And, to illustrate this very point, Jesus made his way to some of the most despised people in the region, the Samaritans.

More than a thousand years before Jesus' time, the ten northern tribes of Israel had rebelled and started their own government, leaving only the two southern tribes of Judah and Benjamin as the "real Israel" under the rule of King David's dynasty. The northern tribes rejected the Jerusalem temple worship and set up golden calves at their own shrines.

Eventually, the Assyrians swooped in and wiped out the northern kingdom, took the people captive, and sent in others to repopulate the devastated area. Later, Judah was also sent into exile. When the Jewish people finally returned to rebuild the temple, they forbade help from, or inter-marriage with, the people of the erstwhile northern kingdom, now called Samaria.

For the next 450 years, Judeans and Samaritans hated each other. The Samaritans built their own temple on their own mountain, Mt. Gerizim, in the historic area of Shechem, where Abraham had originally pitched his tent and Jacob had later dug a well. They only accepted the first five books of the Bible as scripture, rejected the oral law, the Talmud, and all the prophets' writings, and they also worshiped five other deities besides Yahweh. They were a people of mixed background, part Hebrew and part Babylonian, Cuthaean, Avvanan, Hamathaean, and Sepharvaimite, and a mixed religion, reflecting all their various cultural roots (2 Kings 17:24–41).

Now, as Jesus and his disciples arrived at Jacob's famous well, they decided to take a break. Jesus sat down to rest, and the disciples went into the nearest town to buy food, most likely a very unsettling prospect for them as Judeans. They may even have passed by this woman with her water jug as they walked into the town of Sychar. Archaeologists show there was another well in town, but she was walking the extra half-mile out of town to Jacob's well, possibly because of her reputation within the community.

I wonder if it made her feel uncomfortable, at first, to see this lone Judean man sitting on the well she would have to use to draw water. But the Lord loves people, all people. There is no ranking system with God, as though some people are better than others. The Lord Jesus loved this mixed-race, mixed-religion woman of questionable reputation, and he respected and honored her with his own humility and vulnerability. He was thirsty for water, and knew she was thirsty for eternal life.

Read John 4
1. How did Jesus put the woman at ease?

How can you follow his example?

2. From verse ten, what three things did the woman need to know?

   How does this relate to the gospel?

3. Describe the differences between the water Jesus offers and ordinary water.

4. What did the prophet Jeremiah intend water to symbolize in Jeremiah 2:13?

   List examples of what people thirst for that cannot fully satisfy spiritual and emotional longing.

   What did the prophet Jeremiah say would satisfy this thirst in Jeremiah 17:13?

5. In what ways do the following Bible passages speak of water?
   Proverbs 5:15, 18:4_____
   Exodus 17:6, 1 Corinthians 10:4_____
   Psalm 63:1, Isaiah 44:3_____
   Zechariah 14:8, Revelation 22:1_____
   Isaiah 12:3, John 7:37–39_____
   Joel 3:18, Revelation 21:6_____

6. Describe the woman's response of partial belief in John 4:15.

7. How did Jesus help her see her own life issue?

   What has God been helping you to see as your life issues?

8. Link Jesus' statement in John 4:22 with Genesis 12:1–3, Romans 3:1–2, Romans 9:4–5.

9. What kind of worshippers does God seek?

    What did Jesus mean? (See Deuteronomy 6:4, Luke 10:27.)

    How would you describe your worship?

10. What can you learn from the woman leaving her water jar?

    What did she do?

    How is this like Romans 10:9–15?

11. What was the immediate result of the woman's testimony?

    According to Acts 8:4–25, what was the lasting result?

12. What lessons and truths have you learned from studying the Woman at the Well's story?

13. What does this passage reveal about God?

14. How is your character and spiritual life challenged by the Woman at the Well's story?

15. In what ways will you live out what God is teaching you? Be specific.

THIRSTY

Hagar

Genesis 12:10–20; 16:1–16; 21:8–21; Galatians 4:21–31

"Take her and go!" Pharaoh shouted at Abram (whose name was later changed, by God, to Abraham). Disgusted, horrified, and outraged by Abram's deception, Pharaoh refused to suffer his presence for even one more hour. Abram, his wife Sarai and all his entourage would have to decamp and leave that very day, famine or no famine.

Their relationship had begun on amicable terms. Already a prosperous man, Abram had arrived in Egypt seeking relief for his herds and clan from a devastating drought. Pharaoh had welcomed this clearly prosperous leader, with his extensive caravan, into his country. The Egyptian king immediately noticed a beautiful woman in Abram's retinue, whom Abram portrayed as his sister (although she was also secretly Abram's wife). Showering Abram with generosity, Pharaoh secured Abram's promise to bring Sarai (later renamed Sarah) into his royal harem. Among Pharaoh's many gifts was a cortege of servants, including a lovely young Egyptian girl named Hagar.

Incredibly, rather than suffer the expected punishment of death, or at least imprisonment, Abram left with everything he had swindled from Pharaoh—all the sheep and cattle, the breeding donkeys and camels, and all the servants Pharaoh had sent to his household. Included was the beautiful Hagar. Whether by choice, or by Abram's forceful enslavement, these Egyptian servants now became a part of Abram's household and property.

What must Hagar have thought as she found herself hastily packing up tents, loading camels, and waving goodbye to the only home she had ever known? Did she even speak the Sumerian tongue of Abram's people? What would be her prospects now, without family or connections?

Not long afterwards, Hagar may have noticed Sarah's calculating gaze resting on her nubile body, and the young Egyptian girl's destiny poised to take a stunning turn. In ancient times a woman's honor rested squarely on whether she bore her husband children, particularly sons, or heirs. The Code of Ur-Nammu outlined a way for barren women to retain their honor: provide for their husbands a fertile woman through whom he could continue his line. Because Hagar had been enslaved, the child would be counted as Sarai's alone, and be taken away from Hagar.

Hagar had no choice in the matter.

Abram accepted Sarai's proposal, took Hagar, and a son was conceived. But this was only the beginning of her degradation. Soon Hagar would be mistreated, flee in desperation, nearly die in the desert, then ultimately be turned out of her home, a single mother and her child, with only a day's worth of food and water, alone in the wilderness. Yet, near death, Hagar saw God, and heard his voice saying, "I will make your son into a great nation."

Read Genesis 12:10–20
1. How did Hagar become part of Abram and Sarai's household?

   What cultural and religious differences might there have been for Hagar?

Read Genesis 16:1–16
2. How did Abram and Sarai's decision regarding Hagar show a mixture of faith and reliance on worldly wisdom?

   What were the results?

3. What caused Hagar's unhappiness?

   List lessons you could learn from this.

   How have you experienced the results of mixing faith with self-reliance or worldly wisdom?

4. How did Hagar respond to her troubles?

   What were the results?

   What good thing did she risk and might have lost?

   How can her experience help you as you face trouble?

5. Who was the angel of the Lord? Give evidence from this text as well as:
   Genesis 32:30_____
   Exodus 23:20–23_____
   Exodus 32:34_____
   1 Kings 19:5–7_____
   Isaiah 63:9_____
   Zechariah 3:5_____
6. What command given in Genesis 16:8–9 is echoed in Ephesians 5:21?

Read Genesis 21:8–21
7. Compare Genesis 16:4 with 21:9. How did Ishmael sin in the same way Hagar had sinned?

   How did Ishmael make it impossible for both families to live together?

8. Why did God have Abraham send Hagar and her son away?

   How did God provide for Hagar?

How did God's prophecy and promise for Ishmael reveal Ishmael's character traits?

Read Galatians 4:21–31

9. From Romans 7:18, 8:8, Ephesians 4:22, and Colossians 3:9, compare Ishmael as the "old nature" and Isaac as the "new nature."

10. According to Romans 6:11 and Galatians 5:2, why did Abraham have to remove Hagar and Ishmael?

    From Romans 8:14 and Galatians 5:16, what is to happen next?

11. Abraham's obedience brought suffering to Hagar and her son. How does Genesis 21:14–21 help us to trust that God will make all things right as we follow his will?

12. What lessons and truths have you learned from studying Hagar's story?

13. What does this passage reveal about God?

14. How is your character and spiritual life challenged by Hagar's story?

15. In what ways will you live out what God is teaching you? Be specific.

THIRSTY

Miriam

Exodus 1:15–2:10; 15:1, 20–21; Numbers 12:1–16; Numbers 20:1; Numbers 26:59; 1 Chronicles 6:3; Micah 6:4

Egypt was old by the time this story takes place, a magnificent culture of military might, technological advances, great art, and sophisticated society. Even the pyramids were showing signs of aging when Jacob moved his clan, at the pharaoh's invitation, into the land of Goshen.

It is difficult to tell when in history the great exodus took place.[1] One possibility is to count backward from the building of Solomon's temple, recorded in 1 Kings 6:1, which would bring us to a period of history when the Hyksos invaded and conquered the Egyptians.

The Hyksos, called the Shepherd Kings, were a Semitic people who had the same lineage as Abraham. They ruled Egypt for around two hundred years and built their capital city in Goshen. With the current dating of pharaonic kings, it could possibly be during this time that Jacob and his family came to settle in Goshen, where they grew wealthy and numerous.

Goshen was a lush, flat pastureland, not generally used for agriculture, protected on all sides by water and hills, and perfectly suited for Jacob's family business of tending the pharaoh's flocks and herds. However, for all the favor the pharaoh gave Joseph and his family, a natural barrier existed between the Egyptians and the Hebrews because shepherding was considered detestable to the Egyptians.

---

[1] A fascinating theory, which posits a much earlier exodus, richly chronicled with archaeological evidence, can be found in the documentary "Patterns of Evidence: Exodus," directed by Tim Mahoney (2014; Minneapolis, Thinking Man Films), DVD.

In 1530 BC a new pharaoh rose to power, Thutmosis I. Over the course of about ten years he managed to drive out the Hyksos and reclaim Egypt. If this is the timeframe of the Israelites' stay in Egypt, then it would be no surprise that Thutmosis would be unfamiliar with the history of Joseph. He would not have known the God who blessed Egypt through Joseph, and through Jacob's descendants.

By now, the Hebrew people had multiplied and grown strong. This new pharaoh was alarmed, facing a force he was afraid he could not control, but which he also was afraid he could not do without. It seems the economy of Egypt had grown dependent upon the Hebrew labor force. Now, the pharaoh wanted to protect the economic asset of free labor, while also protecting national security. His solution? Brutally enslaving the Hebrew people.

Ancient pictorial evidence depicts Egyptians overseeing Semitic slaves making bricks, hauling, building, and doing other forms of heavy manual labor. Egyptian slave masters with heavy whips and long staffs denoted their rank. Things went from bad to worse as the Egyptians savagely subjugated God's people.

It is against this backdrop we meet Miriam, up to her knees in the Nile, who was probably around eight or nine years old—a third grader. As a member of the slave class, she had likely worked hard most of her little life already and helped her father and mother keep the household going. Yet one day this little slave girl would help lead a nation through the Red Sea, and watch God provide for his thirsty people again and again.

Read Exodus 1:15–2:10, Numbers 26:59, 1 Chronicles 6:3, Exodus 7:7
1. Who were the members of Moses' family?

   What was the birth order of the children?

2. From Exodus 2:1–10, Acts 7:20–22, and Hebrews 11:23, describe Moses as an infant.

What risks did Jochebed and Amram face in keeping Moses?

3. Hebrews 11:23 describes this family's faith. What promises of God did Amram and Jochebed have faith in? (See Genesis 12:1–3, 15:13–16)

4. Describe Miriam's character traits and how they were expressed in this childhood story.

    What did Miriam trust God for?

Read Exodus 15:1, 20–21; Micah 6:4
5. Describe the woman Miriam grew up to be:
   Character traits

   Talents

   Spiritual gifts

   Position in the Hebrew community

Read Numbers 12:1–16; Numbers 20:1
6. How is Miriam portrayed in Numbers 12:1–3?

    What prompted Miriam's criticism?

    Explain whether you think she was right or wrong.

7. What does verse three imply about Moses' response?

    How do you respond when you are criticized?

8. What steps did God take in vindicating Moses?

    How did God show Miriam, a prophet, the difference between herself and her brother Moses?

What did God say was the basis for his special relationship with Moses?

9. What was the penalty for Miriam's attitude and actions?

   Remembering God's character of impartial justice, love, and mercy, why was the penalty heavier for Miriam than for Aaron?

10. How might Aaron have felt when he saw Miriam's punishment?

    As high priest, what would he have had to do, had Moses not interceded? (See Leviticus 13:1–3, 45–46.)

11. According to Luke 23:34 and Hebrews 7:25, how did Moses picture Jesus in his intercession for Miriam?

    What seems to be the lasting consequence of Miriam's envy?

12. What lessons and truths have you learned from studying Miriam's story?

13. What does this passage reveal about God?

14. How is your character and spiritual life challenged by Miriam's story?

15. In what ways will you live out what God is teaching you? Be specific.

FOREIGNER

Rahab

Joshua 2 and 6; Matthew 1:5; Hebrews 11:30–31; James 2:24–26

Situated near the Jordan river, and surrounded by generous springs of water, Jericho was inhabited before cities had even been invented. Called the "City of Palm Trees" for thousands of years, Rahab's home was one of the earliest settlements in the world. Archaeological data traces a continuous history of people living in this city since as early as 9,000 BC.

The word Jericho means "fragrant." In Rahab's day, her city would have been redolent with the scent of incense wafting from spreading plantations of sycamores, myrrh trees, and balsam plants filling the air with their aroma, which the winds blew as far as the Mediterranean coast.

Jericho experienced a regular influx of international travelers as one of the most prosperous cities in the Levant, lying right along the caravan road between Egypt to the south, and Sumeria to the north. Imagine a rich and thriving city, filled with artisans and shopkeepers, money exchangers, vendors offering food and drink, and caravans from every part of the known world. Imagine much good cheer, warmth, and money; as well as the king's soldiers expertly mingling among the people, keeping a sharp and wary eye for any signs of trouble, and an ear to the ground for sensitive information.

Apparently, though her family was also living in the area, Rahab was the head of her own household. She owned a home built against Jericho's inner town wall. It had a stairway leading up to a traditional flat roof home—which dot the Mediterranean even to this day. The roof of her establishment—most likely both a wayside inn and a brothel—would have been just about level with the ramparts and must have been a continuation of the wall itself. It was visible to everyone, for the king seemed to have almost instantly known that two foreign-looking men had entered her tavern. Situated near the gate, Rahab would have had a steady stream of travelers, tradesmen, and merchants visiting her establishment. It is possible Rahab herself kept a side business in textiles, given the evidence of flax on her rooftop.

The Bible does not varnish the truth about Rahab. Both the Hebrew and Greek words for her occupation mean "harlot," though there is evidence she was also an innkeeper and very possibly a brewer. All three occupations were often linked, with brewing (from its infancy) belonging exclusively to women in the ancient Near East.

Either way, Rahab was a woman of her day and of her culture. Canaanites were idolaters, whose morals and lifestyle had become so corrupt God said the very land was ready to "vomit them up" (Leviticus 18:28). God had waited with caring patience until Canaan's sin had "reached its full measure" (Genesis 15:16), but now the time had come for his judgment.

How could an idolatrous, utterly corrupted Canaanite prostitute ever hope to escape God's righteous judgment? Nevertheless, the Lord will always rescue anyone who turns to him in faith; as Jesus said, "whoever comes to me I will never drive away." (John 6:37)

Read Joshua 2:1–24

1. Recount how Joshua was able to get information about Jericho.

2. From verses 8–13, why did Rahab help the Israelite men? (See also Hebrews 11:31 and James 2:24–36.)

   What risks are you facing right now? How will your knowledge of God inform your course of action?

3. Describe Rahab's plan to save the Israelite men and her own family. (Incidentally, the scarlet cord of flax was most likely Rahab's life savings, as it was a way to store valuable dye.)

4. What risks are you willing to take for the salvation of others?

Read Joshua 6:1–27; 1 Chronicles 2:1–11; and Matthew 1:5

5. From verses 6:3–16, depict the battle strategy. How might Rahab and her family have felt during this time?

6. Recount a time when you said or did something because you were trusting God? How did it turn out?

7. From 6:17–19, 24, what were the Israelites to do with the city of Jericho's contents?

    Explain why God gave these instructions from Genesis 15:16; Deuteronomy 12:29–32, 20:16–18; Leviticus 18:24–28; and any other Bible passages.

8. Yet Rahab and her family were spared. What happened after their rescue? (See Joshua 6:22–25).

    Considering Rahab's marginalized background, what does this say about God and his people?

9. Trace Rahab's descendants in 1 Chronicles 2:1–11.

10. From the book of Ruth, describe something of Rahab's legacy in her (great-) grandson.

   How does this reflect on the way Rahab translated her faith into her parenting?

11. From Matthew 1:5, how did God honor Rahab's faith?

12. What lessons and truths have you learned from studying Rahab's story?

13. What does this passage reveal about God?

14. How is your character and spiritual life challenged by Rahab's story?

15. In what ways will you live out what God is teaching you? Be specific.

FOREIGNER

Ruth

The Book of Ruth; Matthew 1:5

Ruth was from Moab, a mountainous region known for its limestone hills, scarcity of trees, and plentiful rain, in what is today the country of Jordan, along the eastern shore of the Dead Sea. It was here, on Mount Nebo, that Moses had gazed into the Promised Land before he died.

Ammon, the nation to the north, and Moab shared the same origin history. According to the Bible, when Sodom, Gomorrah, and the cities of the plain were destroyed, the only inhabitants who escaped that cataclysm were Lot and his two daughters. Fearing they would never marry nor have families of their own, both daughters seduced their father and conceived sons. Ammon and Moab eventually established their namesake nations (Genesis 19:30–38).

Sadly, though these three people groups, the Israelites, Moabites, and Ammonites, all shared similar ancestry, there was no love lost between them, and usually their borders were closed to each other.

However, Ruth's story probably took place very early in Israel's history, in the time of the judges, during a particularly relentless drought when Gideon was judge, possibly somewhere between 1191 and 1144 BC. At this time, a rare, temporary peace existed between Moab and Israel (Judges 6:1–6).

The Bible speaks of a famine so severe that Elimelek, a man living in Bethlehem, felt compelled to take his wife Naomi, along with their two boys, to Moab in search of food. Years later, when their sons were grown, tragedy struck, and Naomi found herself widowed, left only with Orpah and Ruth, the Moabite widows of her dead sons.

Eventually, Orpah returned to her home, but Ruth was willing to give up everything life could hold for her in Moab—a new husband and family, her own people, religion and culture—to be close to God through Naomi.

Ruth is a story of redemption. In fact, that word shows up twenty-three times in this short book of only four chapters. In response to Ruth's great longing to belong to God and to his people, he redeemed her from widowhood and childlessness and placed her in the lineage of his own Son. Boaz, in turn, is called the kinsman redeemer. He offered redemption to a woman who otherwise would have had no hope of marriage and family.

Yet middle-aged Boaz also experienced redemption in marrying a young woman of such depth of character and love. And Naomi experienced redemption from her life of desolation, bereft of husband, sons, and land, through the devotion of Ruth and the kindness of Boaz. Her status was redeemed in society by the marriage of her daughter-in-law to a kinsman, by the birth of her grandson, and by the increase even in her standard of living, no longer gleaning and begging, but living well.

Ruth and Boaz were very ordinary people, a poor young widow from a hostile foreign country, and a plain, middle-aged farmer. Yet, their hearts were filled to overflowing with a love for God and a love for others. This is the heritage God wanted for his Son, the Lord Jesus Christ.

Read Ruth 1

1. From Judges 2:10–19 and Judges 21:25, depict the "days when the judges ruled."

   Define the relationship between the Israelites and Moab. (See Genesis 19:36–38; Numbers 22:1–6; 25:1–9; Deuteronomy 23:3–6.)

2. What prompted Elimelek to relocate his family to Moab?

How long did he intend to stay?

How long did they actually stay, and what happened during those years?

In what ways have current events affected your decisions and your family?

3. Explain what Ruth might have felt and believed when she made her vow in 1:16–17.

What vows have you made to others? To God?

4. What did Naomi believe about God? (See 1:6, 8–9, 13, 20–21.)

What do you believe about God?

Read Ruth 2

5. According to 1 Chronicles 2:1–11 and Matthew 1:5, who was Boaz, and how did he help Naomi and Ruth?

6. Give Boaz' reasons for helping Ruth. (See 2:10–12.)

How else was Boaz kind to Ruth?

How do you think others would characterize the way you are with your family?

7. What did Naomi say about Boaz to Ruth?

8. In what ways was God at work, unseen?

Read Ruth 3

9. Detail Naomi's plan for Ruth. What did Ruth do?

10. What can we learn about Boaz from his response and his words? (See 3:10–17.)

    How do you respond when others ask you for help?

Read Ruth 4

11. What does "redemption" mean? (Use a dictionary.)

    Describe all the ways redemption was worked into the lives of Boaz, Ruth, and Naomi.

    What has God redeemed in your life?

12. What lessons and truths have you learned from studying Ruth's story?

13. What does this passage reveal about God?

14. How is your character and spiritual life challenged by Ruth's story?

15. In what ways will you live out what God is teaching you? Be specific.

FOREIGNER

Herodias

Matthew 14:3–12; Mark 6:12–28; Luke 3:19–20

Herodias' family tree is evident from her name. The wife of Herod Antipas, tetrarch of Galilee, she was also the granddaughter, as well as daughter-in-law, of Herod the Great, who had governed all of Palestine the year Jesus of Nazareth was born. Herod the Great was the man the magi had come to see, asking about a baby and a star. He was also the one who ordered the slaughter of all the baby boys in Bethlehem. It had been no big deal to him. He had numerous sons and daughters of his own, by ten wives, and he had killed them, too, when he thought they were getting in his way. It is actually notable that Herodias had survived his jealous paranoia, when so many had not.

When Herod the Great died, he divided Judea into three portions; then, with Rome's permission, he divvied these portions out among three of his surviving sons. Archelaus got Judea and Samaria, Philip got Trachonitis and Ituraea, and Herod Antipas got Galilee and Peraea. It was at this time that an angel came to Joseph and told him it was safe to move back to Nazareth. A fourth son, named Herod Philip, received money as his portion and lived in Rome.

The year before John the Baptist was beheaded, Herod Antipas went to Rome to visit his half-brother, Herod Philip, and began to admire Philip's wife, Herodias. Who knows who seduced whom, but Herod and Herodias ended up having an affair, and Herod brought her and her teenage daughter Salome back with him to Galilee. One problem—Herod was already married to a princess whose father, Eretas Philopetras, king of the Nabateans, ruled Petra right next door. Regardless of her parentage, however, Herod divorced that wife and deported her to Petra so he could import his new flame Herodias into his palace.

Herodias' marriage to Herod eventually proved disastrous, as the king of Petra would mount a war Herod had no hope of winning. Herodias had also urged her husband to try to discredit their relative Herod Agrippa, which provoked the emperor Caligula's ire, prompting their banishment in 39 AD, and possibly also indirectly causing Herodias' death later that same year.

John the Baptist had boldly denounced what Herod and Herodias had done. In an attempt to mollify his wife, Herod Antipas had imprisoned John, though he would also often visit the Baptist to hear him teach and preach. For the next ten months Herodias nursed a grudge against John the Baptist and wanted to kill him.

Finally, one night, Herodias recognized her opportunity.

Read Matthew 14:3–12; Mark 6:12–28; Luke 3:19–20, 9:6–9

1. Weaving together the three Gospel accounts, retell her story from Herodias' perspective.

2. From these passages and Luke 13:31–33, 23:7–11, characterize Herod.

3. How can someone appreciate a good person, and be interested in what they say, yet still choose evil? Explain.

4. From these passages, characterize Herodias.

Heroine or Villainess?

5. What "poison" was eating away at Herodias? (See Psalm 140:1–3.)

6. From Matthew 5:43–48, describe Jesus' teaching concerning one's enemies.

   What do your relationships reveal about your understanding of Jesus' teaching?

   What might be hindering you from fully embracing Jesus' instruction?

7. What does Scripture proscribe for processing anger? (Use such passages as Matthew 5:23–24, Ephesians 4:26, James 1:19, etc.)

8. What do these Bible texts teach about harboring resentment?
   Job 5:2_____

   Job 36:13_____

   Proverbs 3:11_____

   Amos 5:7_____

   Acts 8:23_____

   Ephesians 4:31_____

   Hebrews 12:15_____

   2 Timothy 2:24_____

9. How would you describe Herodias' moral and spiritual influence on her daughter?

Who were the most influential in your formative years? How did they influence you?

10. What did the apostle Paul mean when he wrote 1 Corinthians 15:33?

    Thinking about Paul's words in 2 Corinthians 10:15, who currently influences you most? What do you admire about them?

11. How would you describe your own moral and spiritual influence on those in your care?

12. What lessons and truths have you learned from studying Herodias' story?

13. What does this passage reveal about God?

14. How is your character and spiritual life challenged by Herodias' story?

15. In what ways will you live out what God is teaching you? Be specific.

FOREIGNER

Esther

Book of Esther

The book of Esther is set toward the end of Judean captivity, taking place sometime in the years between chapters 6 and 7 of the book of Ezra.

There had long since been a remnant of Judeans who had gone back to Judah and rebuilt the temple in Jerusalem when Esther's story took place. The bulk of the Jewish people living in exile did not want to leave their homes in Persia due to all the hardships of moving to and living in Israel. When you think about it, by not answering God's invitation through Cyrus to return to Judah, the exiled Judeans may have placed themselves in harm's way. Yet God still rescued them.

There is some debate as to whether the book of Esther is historical, or written as a play or story, peopled by characters based on historical figures, places, and timeframe. Elements such as the use of hyperbole to describe Haman's gallows, the difficulty in establishing which king—and more notably, which queen—Esther's story describes, and the depiction of a few unlikely scenes (particularly a massive, three-day civil war completely absent from Persian sources) move many scholars to reject its historical validity. It is even argued the festival of Purim began as a Babylonian or Persian festival, celebrated much like Mardi Gras is today, and was later justified by the story of Esther.

Those who do accept Esther as not only a true story, but historical as well, begin with the ancient king of Persia as their proof. There are several men identified in Scripture as Xerxes, or Ahasuerus, a common title, like "czar" or "shah" or "pharaoh." The ancient Greek historian Herodotus described this Xerxes as impetuous, passionate, and the handsomest of all the kings, yet also cruel and despotic.

Esther's story opens with the despotic young Xerxes throwing a months-long bacchanal for all his diplomatic liaisons, kings, and princes, as well as his own noblemen. One drunken night, he demanded his powerful queen come display herself to his array of guests, an invitation she refused. Infuriated, Xerxes deposed her, and began a nationwide search for a new wife.

Perhaps it seems like a Cinderella story. Yet, like every other Judean family with their daughters, Mordecai sought to hide his beloved niece Hadassah. To be summoned would mean her dreams—for a godly husband, a family of her own, the worship of the Lord, the law, the festivals, the promises, her inheritance in Israel—would all be crushed. Each young woman's night with the king, her "audition," would end with him sampling her body as well, and if she did not please him she would grow old in the forgotten recesses of his growing harem.

Jewish tradition adds an epilogue to Hadassah's story of being transformed into the resplendent Esther, Queen of Persia. According to some sources[2], Esther remained Xerxes' queen for thirteen years and bore him a son, Darius II, who would later rebuild the temple in Jerusalem.

Read Esther 1–2

1. Give at least two events from these chapters that reveal God's provision on behalf of his people.

As you look back over your life, what circumstances point to God's provision for you?

---

[2] "Esther ." Encyclopedia of World Biography . . *Encyclopedia.com*. (April 23, 2020). https://www.encyclopedia.com/history/encyclopedias-almanacs-transcripts-and-maps/esther

2. Why do you think Mordecai did not want Esther to reveal her nationality at this point?

   Describe a time when you found yourself in a foreign place, feeling like an exile.

Read Esther 3–5
3. What act of devotion to God triggered Haman's smoldering hatred of the Judeans?

   When have you shown devotion for God in a difficult situation?

4. Explain what the key phrase in the book of Esther, found in 4:14, means.

   How does it show God's hand in Esther's life?

5. Where do you think God has put you "for such a time as this?"

6. What verses describe Esther's:
   Prayer

   Risk of faith

   Patience for God's timing

Read Esther 6–10
7. In what ways did God show Esther when it was time for her to make her request?

8. Portray how Esther showed she trusted God.

9. What securities in life might you be clinging to right now? Are they guaranteed? What happens if they are gone?

   How will you show your trust in God in the coming weeks?

10. Portray the eventual outcome for:
    Haman

    Mordecai

    Esther

    The Jewish people

11. How might Psalm 7 relate to the events in Esther's life?

12. What lessons and truths have you learned from studying Esther's story?

13. What does this passage reveal about God?

14. How is your character and spiritual life challenged by Esther's story?

15. In what ways will you live out what God is teaching you? Be specific.

IMPRISONED

Eve

Genesis 1:26–31, 2:18–4:2, 25; 5:1–2; 2 Corinthians 11:1–4;
1 Timothy 2:13

Most would view Genesis 2 as the Bible's introduction of Eve. In fact, whole theologies have been developed on the supposition that another, unnamed, woman was created in Genesis 1 (later identified as a creature named Lilith) who ultimately rejected Adam as her husband, thus prompting God to create a second woman for the man in Genesis 2. Yet, to discover Eve's beginnings, our introduction to the mother of humankind does come in Genesis 1.

> *So Elohim created humankind in his own image,*
> *in the image of Elohim he created them;*
> *male and female he created them.*

If we view Genesis 1 and 2 as a single creation account portrayed as first an overview and next as a close-up of humankind's story, we see God's great love and joy as he anticipated the climax of his creative undertaking. What was about to happen was so lovely, so stupendous, was such the glorious peak of God's creative acts, that for Moses the beauty of it could only be described in a poem. He wove together the Hebrew verbs *asa*, which is to manufacture from substances already in existence, and *bara*, which is divine creation, creating something entirely new that never existed before.

Humankind was manufactured from the substances of earth. But, there is something new here as well, something that is brought into existence which before did not exist, setting human beings apart from plants, fish, birds, and animals.

Bara is used three times in God's poem. The human, the being with a spirit, bears the image of God. Together women and men would be an expression of God's image, made with a spirit, and able to receive God. The extended creation story in Genesis 2 provides a deeper look at how God brought men and women into being. In this account, it is made clear both humans have come from the same source, the same lump of clay, sharing even the same original breath of life. Having been formed from one substance, the first man and woman would also, in a particular way, be a lasting metaphor of the triune God, for Jesus was of one substance with the Father and the Holy Spirit.

As the three-in-one God is fully divine and fully equal within the one Godhead, so women and men are both completely equal in attributes and character. They share equally in God's blessing; share equally in God's mandate to be fruitful, to fill their world; share equally in developing and governing the earth; and share equal authority in caring for the world. In God's original design, men and women were not to rule each other, but rather, together were to tend and befriend the world God had given them. How tragic for Eve to lose this freedom and become imprisoned by the effects of the fall.

Read Genesis 1:26–31
1. List the work and the blessing that God gave equally to men and women.

    What additional truth does Psalm 8 provide?

2. In what ways do you live out what God has given you to do and lay claim to the blessings he's given you?

Read Genesis 2:18–24

3. Why do you think the Lord said it was not good for the man to be alone?

   From the following verses, describe the word "helper." Who else did the Lord refer to as "helper" in these passages?
   Exodus 18:4_____
   Deuteronomy 33:29_____
   Psalm 10:14_____
   Psalm 118:7_____
   Hebrews 13:6_____

4. What significance is found in the woman being made of the same substance as the man? How might this relate to God's triune nature?

5. Why do you think the man and woman felt no shame in their nakedness? (See Genesis 2:25.)

   Comparing Exodus 34:29, Isaiah 61:10, and 2 Corinthians 3:1–11, 17–18, how might the man and the woman have seen each other?

6. How do you see your brothers and sisters in the Lord? How do you think they see you?

Read Genesis 3

7. What details stand out to you?

   In what ways was Eve deceived, and by whom?

   What additional insight do 2 Corinthians 11:1–4 and 1 Timothy 2:13–14 provide? (Some Bible translations say "blundered" rather than "made a sinner," referencing Romans 5:14.)

8. What light did Eve have, and what did she lose?

   What light has God given you? What are you doing with it?

9. Describe in your own words what God said would now happen to Eve, to Adam, to the earth, and to the serpent. (KJV is the best translation for Genesis 3:16.)

   How have God's predictions proven true?

   How has your own life been affected?

Read Genesis 4:2, 25; 5:1–2

10. Thinking about God's ray of hope to Eve in Genesis 3:15, who might she have thought her son Cain could be?

    How might this have affected Cain, as revealed in his character and actions?

11. How might the people in your care be affected by the way you view them?

12. What lessons and truths have you learned from studying Eve's story?

13. What does this passage reveal about God?

14. How is your character and spiritual life challenged by Eve's story?

15. In what ways will you live out what God is teaching you? Be specific.

IMPRISONED

Daughter of Jairus

Matthew 9:18–26; Mark 5:21–43; Luke 8:40–56

The story of Jairus' daughter is found interwoven with another woman's story—an unnamed woman who had suffered for years from a mysterious illness which not only was sapping her of life, but had impoverished her and rendered her unclean for years. It is evident the Gospel writer intended these two stories to be read as a single unit, for many parallels are drawn between them.

Taking place during the height of Jesus' ministry, he was regularly surrounded by great throngs of people, eager to hear his teaching and—probably even more so—to be touched by his powerful healing hand. In the events immediately preceding the healing of Jairus' daughter and the woman with a bleeding disorder, Jesus had been to Gadara and sent a legion of demons into a whole herd of pigs, which had then run off a cliff and into the sea. The townspeople, rather than being delighted by the restoration of one of their own, were alarmed and distressed over the shocking loss of their income and property. They asked Jesus to leave, which he did.

His next destination was Nazareth, which one might have thought of as Jesus' own city since that is where he grew up. But the people of Nazareth hated Jesus so much they had already tried to push *him* off a cliff! After that episode the Lord had gone to live in Capernaum, where he had begun his ministry, and called his first four disciples: Peter, Andrew, James, and

John. In fact, Peter's home acted as Jesus' "home base" where he often stayed as he taught throughout this region.

So, the story begins with Jesus casting out demons, then was cast out himself, and now is heading to another place where the inhabitants had also cast him out. Several people feature in this tumultuous day in Jesus' life:

Jairus: Synagogue rulers were laymen who looked after the building, supervised the worship, and maintained order. He would be the one to make sure no tax collectors or other unclean persons entered the synagogue, and he would choose who could read from the Scripture scrolls. As a ruler of the synagogue, Jairus was part of the religious establishment which was roundly against Jesus.

A bleeding woman: Imprisoned by her illness, drawn by her intense and desperate need, her presence jeopardized everyone (as you will discover in this study).

Jairus' daughter: A young girl just entering puberty whose life was also ebbing away, soon to be enclosed by a casket.

The professional mourners: Paid performers who made a great religious show without having the spiritual reality.

The wife of Jairus: Left without recourse, alone, and powerless to save her only child.

Jesus' disciples: Most notably Peter, James, and John who would come to witness the most intimate, glorious, and powerful events of Jesus' ministry.

Read Mark 5:21–43, Matthew 9:18–26, and Luke 8:40–56

1. Make as many observations as you can about the "who, what, where, and when" of the stories in this passage. Note the details.

   Try to summarize, in a few sentences, what happened.

2. What details can you find which surround and describe:
   Jairus' daughter

The woman with a bleeding disorder and her healing

The situation at Jairus' house

3. Thinking of this passage as a whole, why is the story of the bleeding woman inserted into the middle of the story of Jairus' daughter?

   Compare the darkness the daughter and the bleeding woman faced. Could either come into the light without God's help?

   What darkness are you facing? Who are you going to for help?

4. Considering the tension between Jesus and the religious rulers, what did Jairus risk in coming to Jesus?

   What were the implications for Jesus, and the synagogue ruler, in this unexpected circumstance? (Leviticus 5:2–3, 5–6; Leviticus 7:21)

5. What risks did the bleeding woman take? (Leviticus 5:2–3, 15:25–27)

   What was her life situation at this point?

   Nowhere else in the Gospels did Jesus call a woman "daughter." With Jairus standing next to him, why did Jesus call this woman daughter?

6. How do you think God views you?

7. Like Jesus, when you have been caught off-guard, or unexpectedly interrupted, how did you respond?

8. What do you think Jesus meant in Luke 8:45–46?

9. Why would Jesus want the bleeding woman to be publicly revealed? (Think of Jesus' disciples and Jairus observing, as well as her own assessment of herself.)

10. What happened during this delay? (See Luke 8:49.)

    When has God's "delay" in your life caused sorrow, tragedy, or calamity?

    Why do you think God allowed it?

11. Link Luke 8:48 and 50 together. What did Jesus want Jairus to understand? (Compare with Jesus' conversation with Martha in John 11:21–27.)

    What might Jairus have known from the earliest days of Jesus' ministry? (See Luke 7:11–16.)

    Describe the experience of Jairus' daughter as Jesus spoke to her. (See Luke 7:11–17; John 10:3, 11:43–44.)

12. What lessons and truths have you learned from studying the story of Jairus' daughter, including the bleeding woman?

13. What does this passage reveal about God?

14. How is your character and spiritual life challenged by these stories?

15. In what ways will you live out what God is teaching you? Be specific.

IMPRISONED

Wife of Potiphar

Genesis 39

Potiphar's wife must have been a woman of some substance, as she had married an ambitious and well-to-do military officer who had advanced to become the captain of the guard. She also would have come from a family of similar standing, with a certain measure of wealth, reputation, and privilege. Marrying well, she lived a life of ease, though no children are mentioned.

There is some question as to whether her husband Potiphar might have been a eunuch. The word *saris*, used to describe Potiphar's connection to Pharaoh both in Genesis 37:36 and 39:1, can sometimes mean eunuch and at other times has been translated as official or officer. Since the nuance of a word's meaning can evolve over time, there is some evidence that *saris* only meant "official" until after the time period of Joseph's story. However, the final editing of Joseph's story occurred when "eunuch" was an accepted meaning for *saris*.

This word might have been chosen to indicate Potiphar was impotent in some other way. If that meaning was intended, it might help to explain his wife's continued advances on a man who had clearly rejected her.

Sexuality in ancient Egypt was open and unrestrained, something like today's hookup culture. Unmarried women seemed free to choose partners as they so desired and enjoyed their love life to its fullest. Interestingly, ancient Egyptians also highly valued fertility and considered sex a sacred act. Among the pantheon of their gods, the goddess Nephthys was pitied for her infertility, whereas her twin sister Isis was revered above all other goddesses as richly fertile. In like manner to Isis, embodiment of the perfect woman, Egyptian women strove to be intelligent, wise, and mystical bearers of children.

However, although unmarried women were free to take lovers, adultery was considered a grave offense. Women were sometimes even put to death for transgressing the vows of their marriage.

Enter Joseph! His career in Potiphar's household held one promotion after another. Joseph found favor with everyone, he was successful in all he did, and his life reflected God's presence and prosperity. No longer wearing the rags of a slave, he had become a handsome, well-built man, wearing the robes of authority.

At some point Joseph was given access and authority over all Potiphar's lands, holdings, and even his home, to come and go wherever and whenever Joseph pleased. As captain of the guard, Potiphar would often have to be away from home on official business. So, it was inevitable that Joseph and Potiphar's wife would come in contact more often, and in ever more private settings. I think she must have been beautiful, sophisticated, and well-acquainted with the art of seduction. She propositioned him, and when he rejected her, she launched a relentless onslaught of enticement and sexual harassment, unable or unwilling to let go.

Read Genesis 39
1. Describe Joseph.

   How was Joseph continually aware God was with him?

2. Describe Potiphar's wife.

   What did she see in Joseph? Why do you think she kept enticing him?

Read Proverbs 2:16–22, Proverbs 5

3. In what ways might Potiphar's wife have shared traits with the adulterous women in these passages?

4. What light did God make available to Potiphar's wife?

   Think of a time when you might have felt something like the adulterous woman. How did God meet you in that place?

5. What counsel is given in the Proverbs passages when faced with enticement?

6. What did Joseph say?

   What effect did this seem to have on Potiphar's wife?

   What did Joseph do?

7. What is taught about temptation in the following passages?
   Matthew 26:41, 6:13_____
   1 Corinthians 10:13_____
   1 Timothy 6:9_____
   James 1:2–8_____
   James 1:13–15_____

8. From the Proverbs passages, Joseph's example, and the above verses, how will you now face what is currently tempting you?

9. What do the following verses say about anger:

J. Guarnieri Hagemeyer

Psalm 37:8, Proverbs 27:4, 30:33 _____
Romans 2:8 _____
Ephesians 4:26, 31 _____
James 1:20 _____

Now angry, what did Potiphar's wife finally do, after repeated rejection?

10. Romans 1:24–25 and 2 Timothy 3:2–4 are stiff indictments against those who reject God's light. How might this apply to Potiphar's wife?

11. The penalty for adultery was heavy. But Joseph was taken to the nicest prison, brought personally by Potiphar. Why might he have shown such mercy to Joseph?

    How did God care for Joseph?

12. What lessons and truths have you learned from studying Potiphar's wife's story?

13. What does this passage reveal about God?

14. How is your character and spiritual life challenged by Potiphar's wife's story?

15. In what ways will you live out what God is teaching you? Be specific.

IMPRISONED

Mary of Magdala

Matthew 27:55–61, 28:1–10; Mark 15:40–47, 16:1–11; Luke 8:1–3, 23:49–56, 24:1–11; John 19:25, 20:1–18

Mary of Magdala, also known as Mary Magdalene, is mentioned fourteen times in the Gospels. In eight of those passages, her name heads the list. In another passage, her name follows next after the Virgin Mary's, and in several places in the narrative of Jesus' life, Mary of Magdala stood beside the mother of Jesus, denoting her position among the women who followed Jesus as his disciples. Mary of Magdala was preeminent among them, surpassed in honor save only by the mother of Christ.

Interestingly, Mary of Magdala had a more significant role at the time of the resurrection than any other woman—or man, for that matter. It was to her the Lord Jesus entrusted the first encounter with him in resurrected form, and to her went the good news to spread to his disciples and followers, making her the apostle to the apostles.

Evidently Mary, a Judean woman, was from the town of Magdala, *Migdol* in Aramaic, meaning "watchtower." Its namesake exists to this day as Mejdel, nestled to the south of the Plain of Gennesaret, where the eastern foothills of Mount Arbel reach towards the Sea of Galilee. Because of this, Mary became known as the Magdalene, or Madeleine. Years ago, my husband and I visited the archaeological ruins of Magdala, and enjoyed the sense of peace and beauty among those old stones.

Today Magdala is one of Israel's most visited Archaeological National Parks, as a growing number of tourists, especially women, are coming to visit the restored first-century synagogue and the complete first-century city around it. As you walk among the ancient structures, you will see remnants of the marketplace and shops, where perhaps Jesus taught when Mary was brought to him, caught in the grip of seven demons. Homes dot the landscape, and along what was once its ancient coast, you might make out what is left of a wharf, the "remains of a once prosperous fish processing industry."[3]

Misunderstanding concerning Mary's identity arose early in the medieval period when Pope Gregory the Great conflated her with Mary of Bethany and the unnamed sinful woman who anointed Jesus' feet in Luke 7. What resulted was a false, but widespread, belief that Mary of Magdala had been herself a sinful woman, an adulteress, or a prostitute.

Though we do not know what her life was like during her possession, the Scriptures hint at a compelling woman, well favored, and warm hearted, once she was released from the demons which held her in torment. She, and her family, were influential in their town and generously supported Jesus in his ministry. Filled with profound love and gratitude to the Savior who had literally freed her from bondage, Mary of Magdala became a prominent follower and believer, present at every important event leading up to and including the cross, as well as the upper room in Acts 1 and 2.

Read Luke 8:1–3

1. What darkness was Mary experiencing, and what light did Jesus give her when they first met?

2. In what way was Mary connected to Jesus' ministry?

   Why do you think she was connected in these ways?

---

[3] "About," *Magdala:Crossroads of Jewish and Christian History,* https://www.magdala.org/about/ (accessed January 2020)

3. What can you learn about Mary of Magdala from these verses?

Read Matthew 27:55–61; Mark 15:40–47; Luke 23:49–56; John 19:25
4. Where was Mary when Jesus was crucified, and who was she with?

   What did Mary do the afternoon of Jesus' death, according to these passages?

Read Matthew 28:1–10; Mark 16:1–8; Luke 24:1–11; John 20:1–10
5. Try to piece together the chronology of what happened the morning of Jesus' resurrection.

   What did the women see when they went to Jesus' tomb?

   What message did they hear?

6. Describe the women's response to the angels' message.
   What did they feel?

   What did they believe?

   What were they told to do? Did they do it?

Read Mark 16:9–11; John 20:11–18
7. What must Mary have done after the women left?

   Why do you think she did that? (See John 20:13.)

8. Describe what happened next.

J. Guarnieri Hagemeyer   69

Why do you think Mary did not recognize Jesus? (For help, see Mark 16:12; Luke 24:13–43; John 20:26, 21:4; 1 Corinthians 15:35–53.)

9. What did Jesus do to cause Mary to recognize him, and how is this connected with a phrase in John 10:1–5?

10. Try to explain what Jesus meant in John 20:17.

11. What great privilege was Mary given to do, and did she do it?

    What was the result?

    How could you fulfill the same privilege today? Be specific.

12. What lessons and truths have you learned from studying Mary of Magdala's story?

13. What does this passage reveal about God?

14. How is your character and spiritual life challenged by Mary of Magdala's story?

15. In what ways will you live out what God is teaching you? Be specific.

TRUSTED

Puah

Exodus 1

Knowing Puah's career helps to know something of her life story. She comes across as down-to-earth and practical, someone who knew right from wrong, but also had a large helping of street smarts.

Midwifery in ancient Egypt was practiced by mostly middle- to low-income women from the servant classes. Often a neighbor, friend, or family member of the mother-to-be, midwives learned their trade through apprenticeships, assisting in boosting fertility, contraception, and prenatal care, as well as births, until they could hang up their own shingle and take on clients. Often, as in many fields of that day, the secrets of their trade were kept within the family business, and midwives' children were married within the midwife community.

Midwife knowledge included several forms of conception control and conception enhancement, pregnancy tests, labor and delivery inducement, and spells to help in all aspects of the birth process. Probably the most remarkable among their techniques was a method for predicting a woman's fertility or whether she was already pregnant and whether she would bear a son or a daughter. Tested in the twentieth century and shown to be more accurate than expected, the woman was to urinate on two small bags, one containing emmer seeds and the other barley seeds. If neither germinated, the woman was considered barren. If emmer germinated, she would have a daughter; if barley, then a son.

Labor and birth most often took place on the cool of a house's flat roof, or within a structure created just for that purpose. Instead of lying down, women in antiquity often stood, squatted, or kneeled to help with the cramps and with pushing their baby into the world. The midwife would position herself between the mother's legs to catch the infant in her hands. Other women would stand on either side of the mother to hold and support her throughout her labor.

Birthing chairs were formed by brightly painted bricks, "decorated with hieroglyphic inscriptions of the owner and painted scenes of the mother, baby, and goddesses."[4] Egyptian midwives relied upon the help of several gods and goddesses to protect both mother and child, bring labor to a successful birth, and bring quick and full recovery for all. Among the midwife's tools were a special knife to cut the umbilical cord and an intricately carved ivory amulet to place on the mother's belly. Sometimes midwives would place a dish of hot water under the birthing chair so the steam could help loosen the mother's pelvic muscles and ease her delivery.

It is against this backdrop of Egypt's luxury, medical sophistication, and wealth that the seamy understory of slavery comes into view, for Puah and her colleague Shiphrah were midwives who serviced the enslaved Hebrews. Egypt's current ruling regime ruthlessly subjugated the Hebrew people, and had recently brought cruelty to new levels, instructing the midwives to exterminate every newborn Hebrew boy. What choices would this woman make, trusted both by the oppressor and the oppressed?

Read Exodus 1

1. Retell the story of how the Hebrews ended up in Egypt, from Genesis 45:4–46:7; 47:1–12.

---

[4] Much of the information in this section, as well as this quote, comes from "Ancient Egyptian Midwifery and Birth," *Birth Supplies Canada, Inc*,
https://www.midwiferysupplies.ca/blogs/ancient-midwifery-blog/295322-ancient-egyptian-midwifery-and-childbirth (written by Allison Thiele, 2002, posted June 3, 2008, and accessed January 2020)

2. What did God reveal to Abraham about his descendants' future? (See Genesis 12:1–3, Genesis 15.)

3. What did the new pharaoh fear, and what was his first strategy?

   How did this affect the Hebrews?

   How was God's prophecy to Abraham fulfilled?

4. When have difficult circumstances actually benefited you in some way?

5. What was Pharaoh's second plan?

6. Thinking about the midwives' actions, what was:
   Admirable?

   Questionable?

   What risks did they take?

   How did their actions affect the Hebrews? (See Exodus 1:17, 22.)

7. What might you have done? How do you respond to similar situations involving conflict in moral, spiritual, and legal issues?

8. Explain whether you think Puah and Shiphrah were Hebrew or Egyptian.

What motivated the midwives to help the Hebrew people?

9. What motivates you to live openly for God, or stand strong in difficult situations?

10. How did God deal with the midwives, and what does this say about God?

11. What do the following passages teach about persecution?
    Isaiah 43:1–4 _____

    John 16:33 _____

    John 17:14–19 _____

    2 Corinthians 1:4 _____

    1 Peter 4:12–13 _____

    1 Peter 5:6–9 _____

12. What lessons and truths have you learned from studying Puah's story?

13. What does this passage reveal about God?

14. How is your character and spiritual life challenged by Puah's story?

15. In what ways will you live out what God is teaching you? Be specific.

Heroine or Villainess?

TRUSTED

Sarah

*Genesis 11–25; Isaiah 51:2; Romans 4:19; 9:9;
Hebrews 11:11; 1 Peter 3:3–6*

Sarah was the beautiful, beloved, . . . and barren wife of Abraham. She started out in life as "Sarai," the "contentious," the "quarrelsome." Raised in a wealthy man's home, in one of the most prosperous and cosmopolitan cities in the ancient Near East, Sarah must have grown used to every luxury life had to offer.

Sarah's home, the ancient city-state Ur of the Chaldeans, controlled what is now Iraq, well south of what one day would become Babylon, and about ten miles (sixteen kilometers) west of the current banks of the Euphrates river. In that day, the Euphrates was much closer to Ur, irrigating its fertile fields. Already two thousand years old in Sarah's time, the city had been founded by farmers in the Chalcolithic period (around 5,000 BC) and grew to become the capital city of southern Mesopotamia for centuries.

Married to her affluent half-brother (they shared the same father, Terah), young Sarai may have thought her husband's name of "Abram" was a good omen for her, for it meant "exalted father." Yet sadly, year after year went by without any children, or seemingly even any pregnancies. In Sarah's day, barrenness was considered a great dishonor and shame. According to Sumerian law, written by the ruler of Ur-Nammu, the city of Ur, childlessness would have been grounds for divorce and remarriage for her husband, or at least for the addition of more fertile women into his harem. Yet Abram, according to the Bible, remained faithful to his one and only wife.

It must have come as something of a shock when Abraham announced to his wife and extended family that a new god, "Elohim," had spoken to him and enjoined him not only to leave Ur, but to leave Sumeria altogether. Until now, like every other Mesopotamian family, Terah's clan had worshiped the Anunnaki pantheon of seven planetary gods: An, Enlil, Enki, Ninhursag, Nanna, Utu, and Inanna. Even Elohim's name sounded foreign and strange! But Sarah put her trust in God and in her husband.

In fact, Sarah's character and faith were going to be put through several severe tests over the course of her marriage, trials that would include long years of travel, homelessness, risk to her life and to her honor, turmoil in her home, even internal soul-searching.

As middle age became old age, the heavy burden of truth bowed both Sarah's shoulders and her will. Finally, she capitulated to the Code of Ur-Nammu's clause, and offered her husband a surrogate to have their child. Yet God had so much more planned for Sarah! In a jaw-dropping twist to the tale, the Lord infused new vitality and whole new chapters into what would have ordinarily been the last, golden years of Sarah's story. From barren to birthing nations, from contentious to courtly, at ninety years old, Sarah's life had only just begun.

Read Genesis 11:10–25:10

1. Make as many observations as you can about Sarah in this passage. Note the details.

Try to summarize, in a few sentences, what happened in the course of her life.

2. From Genesis 12:1–3; 13:14–17; 15:1–5; and 17:4–8, what promises did God give Abraham?

   Was Sarah included? Why or why not? (See Genesis 2:23–24.)

3. Why and in what way did Abraham endanger Sarah? (See Genesis 12:10–20; 20:1–18.)

   How did God protect and rescue Sarah?

   How has God protected and rescued you?

4. Why did Sarah have no children according to Genesis 16:2 and Romans 4:19?

   Describe Sarah's solution, and its results, from Genesis 16:1–16; 17:23–27; 21:8–21.

5. What was God's intention, from Genesis 17:15–21? When did Sarah learn of God's intention? (See Genesis 18:1–15.)

6. Judging from God's response, what was the difference between Abraham's laugh and Sarah's laugh?

   What parts of God's spoken word (the Scriptures) do you find hard to believe? What do you think is God's response to you?

7. Look up the definitions of Sarai and Sarah and give God's reason for changing Sarai's name.

J. Guarnieri Hagemeyer   77

How do these definitions harmonize with the apostle Peter's teaching in 1 Peter 3:3–6?

8. How would God characterize you?

9. What lessons about patient faith can be found in
   Genesis 21:1–7 _____
   Hebrews 11:1–2, 11 _____
   Romans 5:3–5 _____
   James 1:1–4 _____
   How can you live this wisdom out in your own life?

10. Explain what happened in Genesis 21:8–13. Why do you think God affirmed Sarah's request?

    What difficult decision are you facing that God is asking of you?

11. Describe Sarah's final days and why Abraham insisted on buying a tomb for her. (See Genesis 15:18–21; 23:1–20; 25:7–10.)

12. What lessons and truths have you learned from studying Sarah's story?

13. What does this passage reveal about God?

14. How is your character and spiritual life challenged by Sarah's story?

15. In what ways will you live out what God is teaching you? Be specific.

TRUSTED

Wife of Job

Genesis 10:21–31, 36:33–34; Book of Job

The story of Job and his wife is one of the oldest in the Bible, and their time period may very well connect with the Table of Nations listed in Genesis 10. Reading through that list we discover that of Noah's three sons, the last, and most significant, was Shem. Through Shem's five sons and their descendants, according to this record, come the people who eventually settled in the Middle East, the Semites. Some of Shem's descendants are highlighted below:

Eber—from whom possibly comes the word "Hebrew." Abraham, who was really the founder of the Hebrew nation, was six generations beyond Eber, but is identified as an Eberite, or Hebrew.

Elam—Southern Mesopotamia.

Asshur—Assyria.

Peleg—who possibly lived during the time of Babel. *Peleg*, in Hebrew, means "division," but in Greek it means "sea." The word archipelago comes from *archi* (first) and *pelagos* (sea). The Greeks called the Aegean Sea, "the Archipelago," the first sea, drawing the name from this man, Peleg. His time may very well have coincided with the Ice Age, when sea levels were very low and land bridges, as well as narrow archipelagoes, connected most of the continents. This time lasted for a very short period and ended abruptly when the planet's ice sheets rapidly melted and filled the sea. "The earth was divided" could have a double meaning of division of languages of the people of earth, dispersion of people groups over the earth, and division of the earth itself as the land bridges quickly disappeared.

Two names possibly link Job to Peleg's time in history; Shem's descendant Uz is also the place name of the land Job lived in (Job 1:1), and Shem's descendant Jobab could be Job himself, who trusted God and loved him regardless of his circumstances.

As its title indicates, this book centers on the man Job. Living a clearly blessed life, it is assumed Job and his wife were favored by God. Yet, when Job received his bitter blows, losing all he had, including his children, his wife shared in his calamity, just as she had shared in his prosperity—in sickness and in health, for richer or for poorer. Imagine her pain, her anguish, and dismay.

Five trusted people interacted with Job. Four were his friends, one was his wife. Job's wife is never named, and she seems only to have added to Job's troubles. Rather than sympathize with him, dress his wounds, or offer any comfort or empathy, she challenged his seeming inertia and exhorted him to action, instead of continuing in his passive self-pity. She has the shortest speech in the book, and the most startling.

As you study Job's story, watch God's response to each of these people, and pay special attention to what changes from Job's old life to his new. Only one person seems to enter into Job's new life with him. Who could it be, and why?

Read Job 1–2

1. Describe Job's character and life circumstances.

   Describe who someone like Job would have chosen to marry.

   Why did Satan cast doubt about Job's love for, and faith in, God?

2. Depict all that happened to Job and his wife in the next few hours. What was Job's response? (See Job 1:22.) How do you respond when disaster comes?

3. What was Satan's second challenge, and how did it affect Job and his wife? What was Job's response this time? (Job 2:10)

   From Job 2:9, describe Job's wife's emotions and her thoughts on God. Who did she see as blameless?

   Look up the several definitions of the Hebrew word *barak*. How else could you phrase what Job's wife said?

   Explain Job's answer. What did he miss in his response to her? What does this say about his relationship with his wife?

4. What truth did Job set his hope on in Job 19:25–27?

> In chapter 3, Job lamented what had befallen him, wondering why he had been born, only to live through such devastation. In chapters 4–37, his friends engaged Job in a debate as to the Lord's reasons for allowing tragedy and calamity to undo Job's life. Finally, in chapters 38–42, God entered the conversation.

Read Job 38–42

5. From Job 38–39 and 41, find phrases that point to God as:
   Sovereign_____ Creator_____
   All-Powerful_____ Sustainer_____
   All-Knowing_____ Righteous Judge_____
   Ever-Present_____ Good_____
   Eternal_____ Wise_____

6. From Job 40:1–5, what was God's challenge to Job?

   What did Job acknowledge, and why was this appropriate? (See Isaiah 6:5–7, 29:13; Jeremiah 12:2; Daniel 10:15–17.)

7. In Job 40:6–14, what were God's four questions to Job? How would you answer those questions?

8. Compare Job 1:20–22, 2:10, and 42:1–6. How had Job's faith matured?

    Why did Job need to repent? Describe a similar situation in your life.

9. Consider Elihu's argument in Job 34:10–11, implying good fortune is deserved, as is misfortune. What do the following Scriptures clarify?
    Exodus 33:19, 34:6_____
    Deuteronomy 7:6–8_____
    Psalm 86:5_____
    John 1:16_____
    Ephesians 2:8–9_____
    James 1:16–18_____

10. From Job 42:7–9, what did God say about Job's friends? What was Job to do? How did God respond, in keeping with his true character?

    Why did God not rebuke Job's wife?

11. Compare Job 1:1–5, 2:9 with 42:10–17. What one thing did God not replace and why?

    In what ways did Job and his family now prosper, both spiritually and emotionally?

12. What lessons and truths have you learned from studying Job and his wife's story?

13. What does this passage reveal about God?

14. How is your character and spiritual life challenged by Job and his wife's story?

15. In what ways will you live out what God is teaching you? Be specific.

TRUSTED

Martha

Luke 10:38–42; John 11:1–44; John 12:1–2

The Bible's depiction of Martha gives the sense that she was the oldest sister to Mary and Lazarus, trustworthy and solid. (Lazarus may have been the youngest member of their household, yet because he was a male, was paradoxically also the head of their household.) It seems this family had recently lost their parents, as no mention is made of them, yet all three siblings appear to have been young and single, and still living together. Judging from their means, the ability to house and feed Jesus and his disciples, and owning between them at least one full pound of nard—valued at a year's worth of wages—Martha and her household were among the wealthier inhabitants of Bethany. Some scholars surmise Lazarus was the rich young synagogue ruler spoken of in Matthew 19, who eventually did come to faith and become one of Jesus' close friends.

The Gospels tell three stories about Martha. In the first story she opened her home to the Lord Jesus and his disciples who were with him. Tension quickly developed as Martha tried to prepare and serve a meal for her large dinner party. Martha's sister, Mary, sitting among the disciples surrounding Jesus, drinking in his every word, seemed not to notice or care, leaving Martha feeling over-burdened and under-appreciated.

Both loved Jesus. Both pulled out the stops for him. Neither one of them had any complaint about his dropping in with a large entourage. In fact, they both seem delighted to throw open the doors of their home to him. One wanted to feed his body, and the other wanted to feed his soul. One wanted to make sure he had everything he needed, the other wanted to affirm who he was.

Both gifts were beautiful, and both gifts were needed, but it seems Martha was not able to see beyond her own task list and the role tradition had assigned to women.

The next place we see Martha and Mary is at their brother's funeral. Martha, though hurt and disappointed, was yet brimming with a cautious hope that even now the Lord could do something for their beloved brother, and his beloved friend. As she saw Jesus approach their home, she came running out to him and had one of the most theologically deep conversations recorded in any of the four Gospels.

In Martha's final appearance, she was once again serving dinner at a large celebration in Simon the Leper's home, thrown in honor of Jesus. Her brother Lazarus, so recently raised from the dead, was also there. Now working together, Martha and Mary were ministering to the Lord in both the ways he needed, to his physical needs of food, a place to stay, a gathering of caring friends, and safety; and to his emotional needs of being understood, seen and known, and cherished and loved.

Read Luke 10:38–42
1. Using outside resources, describe the effort it took to prepare and serve a meal in Martha's day.

   How many people would she be serving?

   From what you know of first century cultures, what was unusual about Mary's behavior?

2. Why did Martha come to Jesus with her request?

3. What might Jesus' response have meant, in light of his teaching?

Compare Luke 10:41 with Matthew 6:25–34.

Compare Luke 10:42 with Mark 12:29–31 and Mark 14:7.

4. Which part of Jesus' response is the most challenging for you and why?

Read John 11:1–44
5. When Jesus received Martha's and Mary's letter, why did he say Lazarus' sickness was for God's glory?

   How might his words have encouraged Martha and Mary?

   How might your own dilemma be to God's glory?

6. What do you learn about Jesus from the fact he waited two days?

   When have you waited for an answer to your prayer? How has that benefitted you?

7. When Jesus came, how did he show his love for, and involvement with, both Martha and Mary?

8. Describe a time, recently, when you experienced God's love for you, and his involvement in your life.

9. Portray Martha's progress in growing faith, from Luke 10:40 to John 11:21–22.
   From John 11:23–28, show Martha's further growth.

In what way is God currently stretching your faith?

10. What difficult decision did Martha have to make to prove her faith? What decision do you need to make?

11. Looking at the parallel stories of Luke 10:38–42 and John 12:1–2, how did Martha now support and help her sister?

    Who do you need to support and help in their ministry?

12. What lessons and truths have you learned from studying Martha's story?

13. What does this passage reveal about God?

14. How is your character and spiritual life challenged by Martha's story?

15. In what ways will you live out what God is teaching you? Be specific.

SEARCHING

Wife of Pilate

Matthew 27:11–26; Mark 15:1–15, 43–44; Luke 3:1–3; 13:1, 23:1–24; John 18:28–19:38

A Roman wife was expected to bear children to her husband, preferably sons and heirs, and be content with nurturing her family, looking after her home, working on handicrafts, and perhaps studying literature, religion, or philosophy. Families of high standing wanted to marry their daughters as young as possible, sometimes even before the onset of puberty, to ensure her virginity and the legitimacy of her husband's offspring. It became necessary for Roman law to limit marriageable age to thirteen years or older. Heads of household were typically the most senior male (often her father-in-law), and women were subordinate to his authority, as well as her husband's. She could inherit, but authority over her money and her property often (but not always) belonged to a male family member.

Pilate's wife, named in tradition as Claudia Procula, would not have been permitted to attend, speak in, or even vote in, any political assembly. However, as tenders of hearth and home, it was also expected of Roman wives to influence their husbands toward moral and ethical good.

Claudia's husband, Marcus Pontius Pilate, was the sixth Roman prefect, or governor, to rule Judea. He had been appointed by the emperor Tiberius, and governed from 26–36 AD. It is unknown where Procula and Pilate lived for most of the year, but during Passover, Judean procurators had been making it their habit to take up residence in Herod's palace on the temple mount.

Like most Romans, Pilate did not like the Judeans and considered them irrational religious fanatics. Predictably, Judeans did not like him either, because he deliberately did things that violated their law and provoked them. Pilate was not above killing people to accomplish his purposes. The Jewish religious leaders, in turn, regularly threatened to report Pilate to the emperor for his cruelty. At the end of his career in Judea, Pilate was recalled to Rome and ultimately exiled for being particularly savage in putting down what he thought had been an uprising in Samaria. Some historians hold that, after some time in exile, Pilate ended his own life. Imagine the turbulence, pressures, and ultimate tragedy of being his wife.

This year, Pilate had a dilemma. Every Passover six hundred Roman soldiers were sent to Jerusalem as an imperial presence to discourage uprisings. The procurator himself would temporarily relocate his headquarters to the temple mount, into a Roman fort built right next to the temple. As a Roman governor, Pilate was pledged to uphold the law. But as a politician, he knew he had to get along with the people. Still, God had given Pilate plenty of insight, and authority, to do what was right, including an oracle from his wife.

It is not known whether Claudia was accustomed to oracles and dreams. However, having moved with her husband to Judea, it seems probable she knew something of Judaism and of Jesus' story. Was it possible both Claudia and her husband were searching for truth?

Read Matthew 27:11–26; Mark 15:1–15, 43–44; Luke 3:1–3; 13:1, 23:1–24

1. Make as many observations as you can about Pilate's story. Note the details.

   Try to summarize, in a few sentences, Pilate's interaction with Jesus.

2. Add further details gleaned from John 18:28–19:38.

3. Jesus refused to respond to Herod's questions; so why do you think Jesus spoke at length with Pontius Pilate?

4. Write out each of Pilate's questions and Jesus' responses:
   Matthew 27:11 with John 18:33–34 _____

   John 18:35 (Why did Pilate ask this?) _____

   John 18:35–36 (How is this question different from the one in Matthew and Mark?) _____

   John 18:37 _____

   John 18:38 _____

   Matthew 27:13–14 with Mark 4 _____

   What was Pilate really asking?

5. How did Pilate's responses to Jesus reveal Pilate's thoughts and spiritual sense? (John 18:33–38; 19:7–12)

6. What message did Pilate's wife send him? (Matthew 27:19)

   How did her words and actions show her spiritual sensitivity?

   What might this all say about Pilate and his wife's relationship?

7. Describe the various pressures Pilate was facing with Jesus.

8. What eternal choice did Pontius Pilate think he was making?

How do you think God viewed his decision? (Matthew 27:24)

What impact may this event have had on Pilate's wife?

9. Describe the eternal choices of the others who were there that day:
The religious rulers (Matthew 27:1)

The crowd (Matthew 27:25)

Jesus (John 12:24)

10. What eternal choice are you making?

11. What did Pilate have fastened to Jesus' cross, and—in your opinion—why? (John 19:19–22)

12. What lessons and truths have you learned from studying Pontius Pilate and his wife's story?

13. What does this passage reveal about God?

14. How is your character and spiritual life challenged by Pontius Pilate and his wife's story?

15. In what ways will you live out what God is teaching you? Be specific.

SEARCHING

Elizabeth

Luke 1

Elizabeth and her husband Zechariah were both from the tribe of Levi. Zechariah traced his lineage through Abijah, but Elizabeth descended from Aaron's high priestly line. They were what you and I might today call "good people," godly and devout people who would have loved to raise a family. In their day, it was assumed God always blessed good people with children; yet, Elizabeth and Zechariah were deeply saddened by long years of infertility—their opportunity seemed gone.

As a Levite priest, Elizabeth's husband Zechariah had been trained in the Torah (books of Moses), the written law, their wisdom literature and history, their traditions, and their oral law. Ordinarily, to be a priest, Zechariah had to have been the son of a priest and to marry a virgin from within his own tribe. In Zechariah's case, it was probably his marriage to Elizabeth, daughter of a priest, that entered him into the lottery to serve in the temple.

Nevertheless, to serve in the temple, Zechariah would have had to undergo a thorough physical examination to make sure he was clean, pure, and without marks, as well as a background check to make sure he had no hint of impropriety.

Living as they did, in a hill country village, Elizabeth and Zechariah may have been considered country bumpkins and minor players in the temple community. But, when it was Zechariah's turn to sprinkle incense in the

Holy Place—at the center of the temple—he was visited by a startling encounter with the angel Gabriel, who announced the astonishing and glorious news that aged Elizabeth would now conceive. Zechariah expostulated in disbelief—which earned him the Lord's silencing for the next nine months!

Perhaps Elizabeth and Zechariah began to think about the other couples in Israel's history who had experienced this same favor from God—Sarah and Abraham, and the prophet Samuel's parents, Hannah and Elkinah.

For the first five months of her pregnancy, Elizabeth kept inside her home, savoring what God was doing in her life. Watching his wife develop from aged woman to glowing mother-to-be must have had a profound effect on Zechariah's faith, because by the time their son was born, he had fully repented of his disbelief. Carried along by the Holy Spirit, Zechariah prophesied over their new baby, recognizing what a miracle he was.

Elizabeth, John the Baptist's mother, rarely appears in nativity scenes or Christmas card illustrations. She seems like a minor player. Yet, the moment the Virgin Mary received the angel Gabriel's stunning proclamation about her own miraculous pregnancy, the first person she wanted to see, in her search for understanding, was her beloved relative, Elizabeth. A woman of spiritual depth and sensitivity, Elizabeth's warm acceptance and prophetic encouragement were of great benefit to Mary.

Read Luke 1

1. From Luke's preface, explain how reliable his account is of the facts.

2. Portray both Elizabeth and her husband from Luke 1:5–7.

3. From Exodus 30:1–10 and Numbers 16:40, what was Zechariah doing, and why, when an angel appeared?

From Luke 1:19, who was the angel? (See also Daniel 8:16, 9:21, Luke 1:26–37.)

4. What significance did incense have considering Psalm 141:2 and Revelation 5:8?
   How does that speak to the angel's assurance in verse 13?

   What assurances does God give today, when we pray?

5. What was the angel prescribing in Luke 1:14–15? (See Judges 13:2–6 and Numbers 6:1–4.)

6. How did the angel describe their future son's character and ministry?

7. What was Zechariah's response, and why did God silence Zechariah?

   What impact might this have had on Elizabeth?

   What do you struggle with in God's word?

8. From Luke 1:23–25, what was Elizabeth's response? What impact would a late-in-life pregnancy have, both positive and negative?

Read Hebrews 11:1–12:3

9. Think of the author's meaning in Hebrews 12:1–3. Describe Sarah's and Hannah's stories.
   Sarah (Genesis 17:15–21, 21:6–7)

   Hannah (1 Samuel 1:1–2:1)

How might this have encouraged Elizabeth?

Whose stories of faith, in Scripture, encourage you as you persevere?

10. Elizabeth's story became the assurance for the angel's news to the Virgin Mary. What was Mary's response in Luke 1:38?

What is your response to God's purposes in your life?

11. What points do you see in Elizabeth's blessing to Mary? Which point is most meaningful to you?

12. What lessons and truths have you learned from studying Elizabeth's story?

13. What does this passage reveal about God?

14. How is your character and spiritual life challenged by Elizabeth's story?

15. In what ways will you live out what God is teaching you? Be specific.

SEARCHING

Wife of Noah

Genesis 5:28–10:32

Noah and his wife's world had become so evil that God announced his intention to cleanse the earth and begin anew. Imagine what trying to raise godly children must have been like against such a cultural backdrop. Imagine the pressures and obstacles faced by a mother with no place of worship, no godly friends by her side, no spiritual resources outside of her home. She must have lived a somewhat isolated life, both shunned and mocked for her faith in God. Perhaps, out of fear, she may have also kept to herself after having searched for friendship, as it seems women were especially targeted for the basest sort of wicked acts. This is the extent of evil that so grieved God.

Even for people who do not know much about the Bible, the biblical account of a worldwide flood is famous. You can see Noah's ark themes just about everywhere. Tribes in New Guinea, India, Brazil, China, Norway, Mexico, and North American First Nation peoples all have a flood story. Each story tells of a favored family (several stories mention eight people specifically) who survived on a boat, two-thirds of the stories attribute the disaster to humankind's wickedness, and over half end with the survivors landing on a mountain. To date, anthropologists have collected between

250 to 300 such flood stories from various cultures.[5]

But for being so well-known, this passage raises a lot of questions and a lot of controversy: Did the flood really happen? How widespread was it? Was it universal or only partial? Was there really an ark, and was it large enough to hold all those animals? Where did the water come from? How does the biblical account relate to the other ancient flood stories found around the globe? What about the Epic of Gilgamesh? And who, or what, are the Nephilim?

The word Nephilim means "fallen ones." They were described as giants with physical superiority who became famous for their military might. Interestingly, there were legends throughout the ancient world of giants with great warrior-like power, such as the story of Odysseus' encounter with the cyclops in the Odyssey.

Evidently, the people of Noah's day had reached a degree of depravity that threatened to irreversibly contaminate the earth. Hebrew words used here to describe such evil are *shachath*, meaning "morally putrid, totally decayed, spiritually gangrenous, destroyed and wasted;"[6] and *chamac*, which means "seeking to gain through assault, physical attack, cheating and/or oppression."[7] Nephilim were the ultimate example of this spiritual and physical debasement, perversion, and degradation of the human race, which would bring about God's cleansing judgment. Corruption had become so widespread and complete, God pronounced total destruction as the only solution.

Imagine Noah and his wife, as they tried to grasp what that would mean for them.

Read Genesis 5:28–32; 6:9–7:17; 7:23–8:1; 8:13–9:1

---

[5] "World Flood Myths," *Ark Encounter*, https://arkencounter.com/flood/myths/ (accessed January 2020)
[6] *Strong's Concordance*, s.v. "shachath," Blue Letter Bible, https://www.blueletterbible.org/lang/lexicon/lexicon.cfm?Strongs=H7843&t=KJV
[7] *Strong's Concordance*, s.v. "chamac," Blue Letter Bible, https://www.blueletterbible.org/lang/lexicon/lexicon.cfm?Strongs=H7843&t=KJV

1. Make as many observations as you can about Noah in these passages. Note the details.

   Try to summarize Noah's part in the story of the flood.
2. What do you think life must have been like before the flood? (See Genesis 6:1–2, 4–7, 11–12; Matthew 24:37–38.)
   How might that have affected Noah, his wife, and his family?

3. How does culture and society affect Christian families today? What about you and your own family?

4. Describe Noah's character and faith (Genesis 6:9, 22; 7:1, 5; 8:20; Hebrews 11:7).

   What kind of woman would he have chosen to marry?

5. How long did it take to build the ark?

   What else was Noah doing during that time? (2 Peter 2:5)

   How many people believed God would judge the earth?

6. What has it been like for you, when you share the gospel?

7. According to Genesis 7:9–10, how long did Noah and his wife and family wait in the boat before the flood came?

   Why do you think this was? (2 Peter 3:3–5)

8. Who finally shut the door? (Genesis 7:16)

What might that have meant to Noah? His wife and family? The people outside?

9. Try to imagine what the deluge must have been like for the people outside the ark, as well as for Noah and his family.

   How do you cope with others' tragedy and loss? How about your own?

10. Describe the ark and its contents (Genesis 6:15-7:3).

    How long did Noah and his wife and family live in the ark? (Compare Genesis 7:6–11 with 8:13–14.)

11. What do you think it was like for Noah's wife?

    What might have been her responsibilities? (See Proverbs 31 for help.)

    What might have been her role in the family dynamics?

12. What lessons and truths have you learned from studying the story of the flood?

13. What does this passage reveal about God?

14. How is your character and spiritual life challenged by the story of the flood?

15. In what ways will you live out what God is teaching you? Be specific.

SEARCHING

Woman Caught in Adultery

John 7:53–8:11

John chapter 7 provides the context of the events surrounding the woman caught in adultery,[8] which took place during the last few months of Jesus' earthly life. At this time, Jewish families throughout the known world would return to Jerusalem and the surrounding area, build temporary shelters out of leafy boughs and flowers, and live in them for a week to celebrate Sukkot, the Feast of Booths. Jesus was also in Jerusalem, though he probably stayed with his friends in Bethany and went quietly to the feast once it was underway in order to avoid a premature confrontation.

Sukkot commemorated God's provision during the exodus, when the Israelite tribes wandered for forty years in the wilderness. It lasted seven days, beginning with the Feast of Ingathering, celebrating the harvest from all their fields, orchards, and vineyards, the months of toil on their threshing floors, and in their winepresses and olive presses. Considered a Sabbath, the Feast of Ingathering was a joyful thanksgiving of God's largesse. It also symbolized God's salvation to all people one day, when he would gather in all nations to himself. This was the people's favorite holiday, full of feasting, singing, and enjoyment.

---

[8] Most Bibles point out that the earliest manuscripts do not include this story, though Jerome (ca. 383 AD) included it in his translation of the gospels and the Didascalia Apostolorum (ca. 200–250 AD) alludes to this incident. In the spirit of narrative criticism, I have chosen to follow the flow of John's Gospel as it is presented.

There were several groups of people swirling around in Jerusalem.

The locals knew what was going on between Jesus and the religious rulers.

The pilgrims from out of town had heard of Jesus, and remembered him from the last festival, but did not realize he was under a death warrant.

The religious authorities—most notably the Pharisees, teachers of the law, and chief priests, along with their cadre of temple guards—milled about Jerusalem, keenly aware of the city's heightened sense of religious fervor, political unrest, and holiday high spirits. They were searching for a way to contain Jesus.

As Jesus walked through the crowds, he would have been able to hear what these various groups of people were saying about him. His practice was to go to the most public place available, the temple, most likely Solomon's Portico (where he had taught at other times) to preach there every day of the festival. When rabbis taught, they would invariably begin by quoting other famous rabbis and theologians. But when Jesus taught, he would say, "Truly *I* say to you . . . " His powerful authority amazed the crowds.

Each day the religious rulers were frustrated in their attempts to ensnare Jesus. The religious authorities had accused Jesus of transgressing Moses' Law. Keeping Moses' Law was all-important because the benefits of God's covenant with Israel hinged on obeying God's commandments. On each occasion Jesus easily turned the tables on them, exposing the religious rulers for what they were—rule-keepers, seemingly bereft of true love for God or his people.

Finally, one morning the Pharisees and teachers of the law thought they had finally come up with the perfect trap, dragging a woman caught in illicit sexual activity and thrusting her at Jesus' feet.

Read John 7:53–8:11
1. Make as many observations as you can about the "who, what, where, and when" in this passage. Note the details, and summarize, in a few sentences, what happened.

2. What does the "Law of Moses" say about adultery? (See Leviticus 20:10 and Deuteronomy 22:22–24.)

3. How would Jesus' teaching about judgment anger the religious rulers? (See John 7:24; John 8:15–16.)

   What was the trap they set for him?

   Why do you think only the woman was brought and not the man?

4. Why do you think Jesus bent down and started to write on the ground? Why the action, and what might he have written?

5. What do you think Jesus was saying about judgment in John 8:7? (See Luke 6:37–45, and consider the apostle Paul's even more pointed statements in Romans 2:1–5 and Romans 2:21–23.)

   How does this affect your own view of judgment?

6. What might have prompted the oldest members of the crowd to drop their stones first?

7. How do each of the below passages shed light on what Jesus meant in John 8:11?
   Psalm 109:31_____
   Mark 2:10–11_____
   Luke 17:3–4_____
   John 3:17_____
   Matthew 12:20_____

8. According to Romans 8:1–4, why did Jesus not condemn someone who had clearly transgressed God's law?

   What light did Jesus give her, and what darkness was overcome?

   According to Romans 8:5–17, how could Jesus know she would be transformed?

9. How would you define the word "repent"? (Use a dictionary for help.)

   How can you tell when someone has truly repented? (See Ephesians 5:1–18 and 1 John 1:5–2:11.)

10. What have you repented of? What have you left behind?

11. Where might you still be carrying the darkness of shame or a sense of condemnation?

    How might Scripture's words in John 8:11, Romans 8:26–39, and 1 John 1:9 give comfort, courage, and hope?

12. What lessons and truths have you learned from studying the woman caught in adultery's story?

13. What does this passage reveal about God?

14. How is your character and spiritual life challenged by this story?

15. In what ways will you live out what God is teaching you? Be specific.

POWERFUL

Anna

Luke 2:22–38

Anna was of the tribe of Asher, which had traditionally claimed the northern shore of the Mediterranean Sea, bordering the Phoenician city of Tyre, and western and coastal Galilee, as its inheritance from the Lord.

When Jacob gave his blessing, he said of this tribe, "Asher grows fine foods, and he will supply the king's delicacies." (Genesis 49:20 CEB) In fact, the only natural harbor in all Israel was in Asher's territory, then the Bay of Akko, and today known as Haifa Bay, bringing in virtually all of Israel's international trade by sea, and playing host to all the nations of the known world. Even when the Roman port city of Caesarea had been completed, Akko and its surrounding Hebrew ports flourished. With comparatively low temperatures and plentiful rainfall, Asher also had some of the most fertile land in the whole area, with rich pasturelands, wooded hills, and orchards. A prosperous tribe, Asher was well-known for its olive oil.

Anna was also the daughter of Penuel (or Phanuel). Penuel's name meant "the face of God," or "the appearance of God" (*el* means God), indicating she was born and raised in a godly home.

Scripture hints that Anna's family might also have been wealthy, in consideration of the relative wealth of her tribe and her father's godly name. After only seven years of marriage, Anna was widowed, evidently without having had children. When she found herself alone, she had the means to dedicate herself to the Lord, going to the temple to live and serve, and never leaving its premises again until she died at the age of 84 years.

Scripture's record of women dedicating their service to the Lord can be found as early as Exodus 38:8, when women served in some way at the entrance of the tabernacle. Later, Psalm 68 described young women playing timbrels and leading worship with other musicians. Perhaps, because her days would necessarily be spent in the court of the women, Anna taught, encouraged, prayed with, and ministered to the many young mothers who came in for their purification rituals; to families who were bringing their children in to worship; to young sons and daughters as they went through their rites of passage; and to those who were making money offerings since all financial gifts were to be offered in the court of the women.

Anna must have also spent many hours listening to the teachers of the law and rabbis speak on the Scriptures, as she would have been there for every festival and high holy day. She would have become just as knowledgeable as they were in God's word. Interestingly, when Luke described this event in Jesus' life, he spent more time on Simeon, but named Anna as the one God had anointed with the power of a prophet—she is, in fact, one of only a few named prophets in the New Testament (Agabus and Silas are the others, besides John the Baptist).

Read Luke 2:22–38

1. Give as many details about Anna as you can.

2. According to these passages, what are the qualifications of a prophet?
   Numbers 11:25, 1 Corinthians 14:1_____
   Numbers 12:6–8_____
   Deuteronomy 13:1–5_____
   1 Corinthians 13:2_____
   1 Corinthians 14:22_____
   2 Peter 1:21–22_____

3. Portray these Old Testament women prophets (whose words have been included as Scripture).
   Deborah (Judges 4–5)

   Miriam (Exodus 2:1–10, 15:19–21; Numbers 12:1–15; Micah 6:4)

   Huldah (2 Kings 22; 2 Chronicles 34:14–28)

   How might these prophets have been role models for Anna?

   Luke identified only Anna as a prophet. What does this say about her, compared to Simeon?

4. Consider the apostle Peter's choice of Joel 2:28–32 to explain what was happening on the day of Pentecost. (Compare Acts 1:14 with Acts 2:1–4 and Acts 2:16–21.) Explain whether God calls women to prophecy today.

5. Name the spiritual gifts the Lord Jesus bestowed to the church according to:
   Romans 12:1–8

   Ephesians 4:7–13

   1 Corinthians 12:1–11

6. In what ways has the Holy Spirit gifted you, and how are you using those gifts for the good of others?

7. According to Leviticus 12:1–8, why were Mary and Joseph at the temple?

What might this have revealed about Mary and Joseph's devotion to God?

How old was Jesus at this point?

8. Why might Anna and Simeon have been expecting to see the Messiah in their lifetime? (Compare Daniel 9:24–27 with Matthew 2:1–6. Daniel was written in Persia, during the Israelite exile.)

Describe how Anna and Simeon both grasped the significance of Mary and Joseph's infant son.

9. What four things did the Holy Spirit reveal to Simeon? (See Luke 2:34–35.)

10. What are some ways Simeon's remarkable prophecy came true?

In what ways did Anna affirm Simeon's prophecy and encourage young Mary and Joseph?

11. Anna waited a long time to have her desire fulfilled. How long have you been waiting for God to answer your prayer and how can Anna's story encourage you?

12. What lessons and truths have you learned from studying Anna's story?

13. What does this passage reveal about God?

14. How is your character and spiritual life challenged by Anna's story?

15. In what ways will you live out what God is teaching you? Be specific.

POWERFUL

Witch of Endor

1 Samuel 28

The Witch of Endor, though she occupies a full chapter in Scripture, and in Saul's biography, seems shrouded in mystery. Who was she—an Israelite or a Canaanite? Had she given up her former ways, or had she continued to practice necromancy in secrecy? Was she well known because she was well liked or because of some sense of notoriety? Did she actually have the spiritual potency of a necromancer, or was some other force or action at work in what she did?

What Scripture does reveal about her has to do with her character, her power, and her response to Israel's king.

Only forty years previously, during the time of the judges, a delegation of Israel's tribes had assembled before the last judge of Israel, the prophet Samuel.

For four hundred years God's people had lived in a loose confederation of their twelve tribes with God as their sovereign, God's law as their government, and the judges as their champions. Because of their small population, Israel had not been able to lay full claim to the land God had given them, despite their miraculous early victories under Joshua's leadership. What is more, the people had often drifted from God's statutes and commandments so that the writer of Judges noted at regular intervals, "all the people did what was right in their own eyes." (See Judges 17:6 and 21:25 for examples.) It can be presumed the people regularly fell into the worship of local gods and into the local cultural practices of their day—the very activities God despised and denounced.

But now, with the growing Philistine threat, Israel had decided they wanted a king like other nations had. What the people were asking for, in essence, represented rejection of God as king and Samuel and his sons as their leaders. But, God was neither dismayed nor without a plan. The Lord was concerned both for his kingdom and for the twenty-year-old man Saul—whom God had selected to be Israel's new king—when God led Saul into the town of Ramah to meet Samuel.

As prophet, Samuel could see Saul had many winning qualities to endear him to the people of Israel as their first king. As judge, Samuel approved Saul's family connections, size, and strength. Yet the first thing Saul said about himself to Samuel was "I'm from the smallest tribe and from the least of all the clans." (See 1 Samuel 9:21.) A nobody.

The whole rest of Saul's life hinges on what was in his heart when he said this to Samuel. For all his good characteristics, Saul felt he had no significance. In the end, Saul was willing to compromise his integrity to shore up his flagging sense of insecurity by visiting the enigmatic Witch of Endor, who by reputation was preeminent among those with the capacity to speak with the spirits.

Read Exodus 7:11, 22:18; Deuteronomy 18:9–14 and Leviticus 19:26

1. Locate Endor on a map of ancient Israel. What other places were nearby?

   From Joshua 17:11–12, what tribe was to settle in this area? How successful were they?

2. Use a dictionary to define:
   Necromancer_____
   Soothsayer_____
   Sorcerer_____
   Augury_____

Divination_____

3. Explain why God forbade these practices. From 1 Samuel 28:3, how had Saul reacted to God's command?

4. Give as many details as you can about who the Witch of Endor was. Explain whether you think she exercised real spiritual power.

Read 1 Samuel 28

> *Saul accomplished some good during his reign, yet he steadily declined spiritually, mentally, and emotionally, as David grew stronger. Now, at the end of his reign, Saul was facing a battle that terrified him.*

5. What situation were David and Saul facing, from opposite sides?

6. From 1 Samuel 28:6, to whom did Saul go for guidance, and what were the results? How has your experience compared to Saul's?

   From your understanding of the time of the judges, explain Saul's final request, and how his servants could answer him so readily.

7. Why was the woman living in Endor so concerned about Saul's request? (For help, compare 1 Samuel 28:3 with Leviticus 19:31, 20:6, 27 and Deuteronomy 18:9–14.)

   How did Saul reassure her? Compare his words to God's command in Exodus 20:7.

   Do you think God honored Saul's promise? Why, or why not?

8. Explain what the Witch of Endor agreed to do and why.

When (and why) are you tempted to set aside your principles? What were the results?

9. Describe the Witch of Endor's discernment in 1 Samuel 28:
   verses 11–12 _____
   verse 13 _____
   verse 14 _____
   verse 20 _____
   verses 21–22 _____
   verses 34–35 _____

10. What did the woman seek to do for Saul? Compare the Witch of Endor's actions to God's instructions to his people in Leviticus 19:18. What does this say about her character?

    What do your actions towards those in need say about your character?

11. How does Saul's story end, according to 1 Samuel 31 and 1 Chronicles 10?

12. What lessons and truths have you learned from studying the story of the Witch of Endor?

13. What does this passage reveal about God?

14. How is your character and spiritual life challenged by the Witch of Endor's story?

15. In what ways will you live out what God is teaching you? Be specific.

POWERFUL

Jezebel

> 1 Kings 16:29–33; 18:4, 13, 19; 19:1–2; 21:1–29; 22:51–53;
> 2 Kings 3:1–2, 13; 9:4–10, 22, 30–37

Jezebel, whose name uses a derivative of the god Ba'al's name (*bel* = Ba'al), was the daughter of the priest-king Ethbaal, who ruled the Phoenician cities of Tyre and Sidon, now the coast of southern Lebanon. In Jezebel's day, Tyre and Sidon were closely related to the city of Akko, officially within the borders of God's land grant to the tribe of Asher, but never actually enfolded into the nation of Israel. King David, centuries earlier, had forged diplomatic ties with Tyre, and Solomon had extended the relationship into a strong economic partnership, exchanging the area surrounding Akko for timber to build his temple and palace.

The Phoenicians were well-known for their diplomacy, open trade agreements, wealthy port cities, and their export of the highly prized Tyrian purple dye. A sophisticated, largely peaceable culture, the Phoenicians enjoyed amicable relations with Egypt, Greece, north Africa, and their other coastal connections, but had recently been invaded and annexed by Assyria.

Meanwhile, after the breakup of Judah and Israel during the reigns of Rehoboam and Jeroboam, Tyre and Sidon retained their alliance with Israel (the northern kingdom), which bordered their territory on the south. The political situation preceding Jezebel's future husband Ahab's reign in Israel was filled with upheaval, betrayals, assassinations, and military coups. One usurper after another, each more wicked than the last, would bring mayhem and bloodshed to the capital city, taking over the throne only to relinquish it mere months, or even weeks, later.

General Zimri was a typical example. He had just taken possession of the palace to begin his reign of seven short days, when he heard that Omri (Ahab's father) had been made king by an uprising of the people. He panicked at the news that General Omri, along with the whole army of Israel, was on his way to establish his rule. No one knows why, but to his doom Zimri set the palace on fire, burning it down to the ground with himself inside. The new king Omri consolidated his power, purchased the lush region of Samaria, and established a new capital city for Israel. Renowned for his diplomatic acumen, magnificent buildings, and legendary prosperity, his nation became known by his own name. Consider the shoes Ahab had to fill!

Most likely it was Omri's diplomatic and political capital that gained Ahab's advantageous marriage treaty with Phoenicia. Jezebel came to Israel as a powerful princess in her own right, bringing with her Phoenicia's wealth, international ties, lucrative trade relations, and even more importantly, added military buffer between Israel and Assyria. Imagine Israel's reception of Jezebel, who was also a deeply religious person; yet priestess of *her* nation's gods, particularly Ba'al and Astarte. It would one day prove her tragic end.

Read 1 Kings 16:29–33; 18:4, 19; 19:1–2; 2 Kings 9
1. Make as many observations as you can about Jezebel in these passages. Note the details.

Try to summarize in a few sentences what happened over the course of her life.

Read 1 Kings 21:1–29

2. One story which defines both Ahab and Jezebel's marriage as well as their characters is found in 1 Kings 21:1–29. Make as many observations as you can on this passage. Note the details.

3. What did Jezebel do and why? Describe her character, influence, and political ability.

   What did this episode reveal about Ahab's character and spiritual life? How might this have affected his reign as king?

4. In what ways did Ahab and Jezebel transgress God's commandments?
   Deuteronomy 5:7 _____
   Deuteronomy 5:8–10 _____
   Deuteronomy 5:11 _____
   Deuteronomy 5:17 _____
   Deuteronomy 5:19 _____
   Deuteronomy 5:20 _____
   Deuteronomy 5:21 _____

5. Portray life under Ahab's and Jezebel's reign.

6. Who inspires you? What effect does their influence have on your character and your actions?

7. What laws of God concerning parenting did Ahab and Jezebel have access to? (Numbers 14:18; Deuteronomy 6:1–9; Proverbs 22:6)

   What effect did these laws seem to have on Ahab and Jezebel's family?

8. Depict Ahab and Jezebel's two sons who reigned over Israel, including the length and character of their reigns (1 Kings 22:51–53; 2 Kings 3:1–2, 13).

9. Portray Ahab and Jezebel's daughter (2 Kings 8:18, 26–27; 11:1–3, 13–15, 20; 2 Chronicles 24:7).

10. What legacy and lasting memory did Ahab and Jezebel leave?

11. In what ways do you influence your family, your friends, and the people you work with?

    What legacy do you hope you will leave? How are you working towards that aim today?

12. What lessons and truths have you learned from studying Jezebel's story?

13. What does this passage reveal about God?

14. How is your character and spiritual life challenged by Jezebel's story?

15. In what ways will you live out what God is teaching you? Be specific.

POWERFUL

Lydia

Acts 16

Lydia was most likely born into a Greek nobleman's home and raised in the wealth and bustle of Thyatira, a Turkish city world-renowned for its dye and textile trade. In fact, Thyatira was home to more artisans and guilds than any other city of its day, including the dyes guild, of which Lydia undoubtedly later became a member.

Most highly valued was Tyrian purple (also called royal purple or imperial purple), first developed in the Phoenician city of Tyre, and later exported to coastal cities to the south, such as Sidon and Akko, as well as Thyatira, inland to the northwest. The dye was extracted from the mucus of tiny Murex snails, varying in color based on the sex and species, then stored and transported in special containers called *amphoriskos*. This dye was worth its weight in silver, and in later times only the emperor himself could wear clothing dipped in this precious and costly color.

An outlier in her time, Lydia made a name for herself in the Tyrian purple dye trade, establishing her own business and household, and enjoying a level of empowerment and independence only a small minority of women in her day were able to experience. Somehow Lydia must have come in contact with a number of the many Jewish people who lived in Thyatira, for she seems to have developed a longing to know the one true and living God.

At some point in her life, for undisclosed reasons, Lydia made the unusual decision to leave her family homestead and business connections and relocate her business to another wealthy town, Philippi. Located in the foothills of Mt. Orbelos in Greece, Philippi was actually a Roman colony, a "Rome away from Rome." Settled by mostly retired military and their families, its citizens were rewarded with not having to pay taxes so long as they remained loyal to Rome, obeyed all the laws of Rome, and kept a basically Roman presence in this conquered area of the empire. Once there, Lydia seems to have sought out the company of Jewish women with whom she could celebrate Shabbat as an adherent of Judaism.

The apostle Paul's pattern was to bring the gospel "to the Jew first, and then the Gentile." But when Paul and his companions arrived in Philippi, they discovered the Jewish community there was so small they had no synagogue. Ever resourceful, Paul knew the Jewish custom was to locate synagogues outside the walls of Gentile cities and somewhere near water, for ritual purification. So Paul led his team through the city gate to the bank of the Gangites River, about a mile and a half outside of town.

To his surprise, he saw a group of devout Jewish women—most likely the wives and daughters of retired Roman soldiers—and at least one God-fearing Gentile (the notable Lydia) who were gathered there to worship and pray.

Without a thought to tradition or propriety, Paul and his companions straightaway sat with these godly women, prayed, and worshiped with them, then proclaimed the life-giving news of the gospel.

Read Acts 16:6–40

1. Make as many observations as you can about the "who, what, where, and when" of the stories in this passage. Note the details.

   Try to summarize in a few sentences what happened.

2. Locate Thyatira and Philippi on a Bible map.

   What would it have taken for Lydia to relocate her household?

Why might she have moved?

3. Why did Paul and his team go to Philippi? (See verses 6–10.)

    What were they expecting? What did they find?

    What does this tell you about God's guidance?

4. Recount a time when you received guidance from God and followed it.

5. Describe Lydia (think of her wealth, her status, her character).

6. What led to Lydia's conversion?

    What was Paul's part?

    What was her part?

    What was God's part?

7. Read Acts 16:15. What did Lydia urge, how did Paul respond, and why?

    What must that have been like for Lydia, her household, and the newly planted church within her home?

8. What kind of spiritual darkness is described in the events of verses Acts 16:16–39?

    How might these events have affected Lydia and her business?

(Consider Lydia's high standing in the community, well known in the business district.)

9. In what ways has your commitment to follow Jesus been affected by what happens to the people in your life?

10. How did Lydia's faith, influence, and generosity impact the early church? (Philippians 1:3–11; 4:10–19)

11. What impact do you have on your church?

12. What lessons and truths have you learned from studying Lydia's story?

13. What does this passage reveal about God?

14. How is your character and spiritual life challenged by Lydia's story?

15. In what ways will you live out what God is teaching you? Be specific.

INTIMATE

Mary of Bethany

Matthew 26:6–13; Mark 14:3–9; Luke 10:38–42; John 11:1–46, 12:1–11

Portrayed as young, single, wealthy, well-known and well-connected with the religious leaders in Jerusalem, Mary of Bethany's biography remains one of the Bible's more intriguing stories. Now known by the Arabic name al-Eizariya, her hometown of Bethany lay nestled in the hills surrounding the holy city, just one and a half miles (about two kilometers) away from Jerusalem—a mere hour's walk, at most.

The Gospels actually tell three stories about Mary. In the first story, the Lord Jesus, along with his disciples, evidently had arrived unexpectedly to the home Mary shared with her sister Martha and her brother Lazarus. While Martha bustled about trying to pull together some kind of meal for all these unanticipated guests, Mary just wanted to be with Jesus, receive his teaching, maybe even just take in his presence, listen to his voice, and watch his beloved face. Whereas it was true in conservative homes that women were to busy themselves with food preparation, and were to serve the men their meals separately, Mary may have hoped that Jesus, who seemed to upend traditional practices on a regular basis, would make room for her. And so he had, for Jesus was pleased to add this woman to those who would be his circle of disciples and followers.

So few people really listened to Jesus, let alone believed him. Even his own disciples did not listen that well, later admitting their hearts had sometimes been hardened (Mark 6:52). Jesus often talked about the people's calloused hearts, not listening, not understanding (Matthew 13:15), and about the religious leaders—who should have been among Jesus' most ardent supporters—having hard hearts (Mark 10:5). The apostle John even said Jesus "would not entrust himself to them, for he knew all people" (John 2:24). Yet, in this first story it is clear Jesus entrusted himself to Mary.

In the second story, Jesus arrived, seemingly too late, to attend to the now dead and buried Lazarus. From her weeping and injured tone with Jesus, it seems evident Mary felt wounded and disconsolate, even devastated by Jesus' slowness in coming. Had he not loved Lazarus or her? Had he not cared what harm his delay would cause? Even still, at Martha's prompting, Mary came to Jesus and shared her tears of grief and broken heart with him.

Remarkably, as expressed in the shortest verse in Scripture, Jesus was so moved he also shared his tears with her: "Jesus wept" (John 11:35).

Yet, it is in the Gospel's final portrayal of her that Mary's story is immortalized. She proved herself the only one among all Jesus' followers—including the twelve—who had been taking in Jesus' predictions. She alone understood at least something of what Jesus would be facing in just a few days' time. Jesus was so deeply moved by her act of sacrifice, love, and discernment, he said her story must be told whenever the gospel is taught.

Read Luke 10:38–42

1. Try to describe the differences between the sisters, their age order, character, demeanor, priorities, etc.

   Mary   Martha

2. What was Martha's complaint, and why did she go to Jesus? How did Jesus respond? What made Mary's choice "better"?

3. What significance was attached to a woman sitting among the disciples?

4. When have you been torn between "many things" and the need for time with the Lord? What do you do?

Read John 11:1–46
5. Why did Jesus delay his arrival?

6. Describe Jesus' interaction with Martha and with Mary.

   From John 11:32–35, depict the level of empathy and emotional bond between Mary and Jesus.

   Can you remember a specific situation when you felt Jesus' love and involvement in your life?

7. Think about the impact of Jesus' prayer and of his raising of Lazarus. What would Martha have told Mary after everyone had gone?

   How might this have affected Mary's love for, and faith in, Jesus?

Read Matthew 26:6–13; Mark 14:3–11; John 12:1–11
8. What should all the disciples have understood by this time? (See Matthew 16:21–28, 17:22–23, 20:17–19; Mark 8:31–33, 9:30–32; Luke 9:22–27.)

9. From all three Gospel passages:
   Describe the dinner scene with as many details as you can see.

Portray Mary's wisdom and spiritual attunement.

How did Mary show Jesus the best of what it means to be a believer? How do you show your devotion to the Lord?

10. From all three Gospel passages:
    What did Judas say?

    What was his real reason for saying it?

    What did the other disciples do?

    How might this have affected Mary?

11. List phrases that showed Jesus' pleasure in Mary's action. In what ways did she minister to Jesus?

12. What lessons and truths have you learned from studying Mary of Bethany's story?

13. What does this passage reveal about God?

14. How is your character and spiritual life challenged by Mary of Bethany's story?

15. In what ways will you live out what God is teaching you? Be specific.

INTIMATE

Virgin Mary

Matthew 1–2, 12:46–50, 13:55, 27:55–56; Mark 3:20–21, 15:40–47, 16:1–8; Luke 1–2; John 2:1–12, 19:25–27; Acts 1:14

It is a pivotal point in Matthew's and Luke's tellings of Jesus' story. Why a virgin birth? Was there a biological reason? A moral reason? A spiritual reason? All we can say is that, from the beginning, God said the deliverer would come from the seed of the woman (Genesis 3:15). This is the way God had always planned to give the world the Messiah.

The Bible describes Mary as a maiden, *parthenos* in Greek, betrothed but not yet married. A godly young woman and devout, she was full of love for the Lord and wise beyond her years. Though the Bible does not give us much on her family background, Luke records her hometown as Nazareth, and later explains both Joseph and Mary left Nazareth for Bethlehem in response to a census. Because Joseph was a builder (the word translated "carpenter" from the Greek actually means a general builder, one who works both with stone and wood—a construction worker we might say today), Mary most likely came from the same economic bracket, a working-class family. They had enough money to secure a donkey for their journey, but so few belongings that they were able to carry the rest with them.

Mary wondered in genuine puzzlement when the angel Gabriel came to announce the conception of God the Son within her. How would this come about, seeing as she was a virgin? The angel Gabriel's description of the overshadowing Holy Spirit seemed to make sense to Mary, but it has left the rest of us, over these ensuing millennia, with our jaws dropped.

God's power to open barren wombs in the stories of Hannah and the Shunamite woman brought believers hope. In Sarah's story, God's miraculous "resurrection" of aged bodies long beyond child-bearing ability had already rocked centuries of believers. But now God was going to bring something out of nothing by his incalculably mighty power—himself in human form.

Mary understood much of who this Son would be, and what destiny lay before him. When she rushed to Elizabeth, the only person who could come close to understanding what was about to happen, Mary was filled with the Holy Spirit and broke forth in prophetic song. How often must Mary have sung her Magnificat to her tiny son, as his lullaby? How often had she reminded him of who his Father truly was, and who he truly was?

Raised in a home which loved and honored God, with parents who took seriously God's command to teach their children all of God's words, even to "talking about them when you sit at home and when you walk along the road, when you lie down and when you get up" (Deuteronomy 11:19), Jesus would come to fulfill the destiny his mother described, and echo the words of Mary in his own teaching.

Read Matthew 1–2 and Luke 1–2
1. From Luke 1:26–38:
   How did Mary show her faith? Give her words.

   What lesson do you learn from this?

2. Of whom do both Matthew and Luke say Jesus was born, besides Mary? Connect with Genesis 1:2 and Job 33:4.

3. List phrases from Mary's song which reveal her:

Spiritual state

Emotional state

Understanding of who God is

Understanding of who Jesus would be

4. Try to put yourself in Mary's place. What might it have cost her in the following particulars to receive this great blessing from God?
Single and pregnant

Birth in a stable, the shepherds, and magi

Flight to Egypt

Read Matthew 12:46–50; Mark 3:20–21; Luke 2:22–52; John 2:1–12
5. From Luke 2:22–40, what did Mary learn about Jesus? How might this have affected her parenting?

How does Luke 2:41–52 reveal the way Mary and Joseph had been raising their son?

6. From John 2:1–12, think about Mary's frame of mind. Explain whether she was in tune with Jesus.

Did her stance change? Explain.

7. Compare Mark 3:20–21 with Matthew 12:46–50 and Matthew 13:55. Why had Mary and her sons come to Jesus?

How did Mary show a lack of understanding about Jesus' person and mission?

When have you wrongly judged a situation?

8. What do you learn from Mary's experiences?

    How might you live out what you have learned in a situation you are in right now?

9. From Matthew 27:55–56, Mark 15:40–47, and John 19:25–27: Where was Mary and who was she with when Jesus was crucified?

    Skim all four Gospel accounts. What did Mary see and hear?

    What did Jesus do to comfort Mary? (See John 19:25–27.)

10. Where was Mary when Jesus rose again? (See Matthew 28:1 and Mark 16:1–8.)

11. What can you learn about Mary and Jesus' family from Acts 1:14?

12. What lessons and truths have you learned from studying the Virgin Mary's story?

13. What does this passage reveal about God?

14. How is your character and spiritual life challenged by the Virgin Mary's story?

15. In what ways will you live out what God is teaching you? Be specific.

INTIMATE

Delilah

Judges 16

Delilah (whose name is a play on the Hebrew word *layla*, meaning "night") overcoming Samson, the mighty sun (in Hebrew Samson is Shimshon, similar to *shemesh* for "sun,")[9] featured early in Israel's history, roughly three thousand years ago during the time of the judges.

Her people, the Philistines, had descended from a group known as the Sea Peoples, who had come down from the Aegean Sea to carve out an existence along the Mediterranean coastline. Philistia's confederacy of five city-states—the Pentapolis of Gaza, Ashkelon, Ashdod, Gath, and Ekron—was located on a narrow strip of coastland bordering the tribal territories of Judah and Dan, now known as the Gaza Strip.

Coming from Mycenean roots, Delilah would have worn elaborately decorated and form fitting clothing, been richly bedecked with jewelry, and kept her hair long, the curls flowing over her shoulders. As the textile industries were mostly owned and run by women during this time period, it comes as no surprise Delilah had her own loom and weaving equipment. Moreover, as a Philistine woman, Delilah seemed to enjoy more autonomy than women in the surrounding cultures.

Samson was born to the tribe of Dan in the town of Zorah, not far from Jerusalem. In Samson's day, the Philistines retained their military edge

---

[9] J. Cheryl Exum, "Delilah," *The Encyclopedia of Jewish Women,* (Jewish Women's Archive), https://jwa.org/encyclopedia/article/delilah-bible (accessed January 2020).

with more sophisticated war technology, including the secret of forging iron.[10] Skirmishes were inevitable as the tribes of Israel continued with God's mandate to clear their promised land of all other people groups in order to claim their inheritance from the Lord.

In the constant upheavals of war and consequent subjugation, God would raise up judge after judge to bring Israel victory, conquest, and a period of peace. Each of these judges was a unique blend of the unexpected, the unusual, sometimes the unconventional, and often the unorthodox. But they all received God's call, empowering, and affirmation, including Samson, the hot-headed, impulsive, womanizing judge in Delilah's tale.

The Bible depicts Philistines as pleasure-loving, warlike, treacherous, and cruel. Philistines did not practice circumcision. The earliest Philistine artifacts reflect an emphasis on female gods.[11] Even to this day, the word lingers as a description of someone who has no manners or taste, a materialistic boor who blunders through social settings like a bull in a china shop.

Yet their material culture reveals a great appreciation for color and beauty, delicacy in their pottery ware, sophistication in their dress and military acumen, and a canny tenacity in their assessment of political terrain. They were able to wrest Canaan from both the Egyptians' and the Hittites' hold, and succeeded in maintaining their own governance for centuries before being assimilated into the local people groups.

In the same way, it seems, Delilah represented her people well in her shrewd triumph over Israel's judge.

Read Judges 13, Numbers 6

---

[10] "Judah took Gaza with its territory, Ashkelon with its territory, and Ekron with its territory. The Lord was with Judah, and he took possession of the hill country, but could not drive out the inhabitants of the plain, because they had chariots of iron." Judges 1:18–19 (NRSV)

[11] Trude Dothan, "What We Know About the Philistines," (Biblical Archaeology Review 8:4, July/August 1982), https://www.baslibrary.org/biblical-archaeology-review/8/4/1 (accessed January 2020)

1. Who delivered these instructions? (See Genesis 16:7–11; Exodus 3:2; Numbers 22:22–35; Judges 2:1–4; Judges 6:11–12, 21–22.)

2. What was a Nazirite, and how was the vow completed? (See Numbers 6:13–20.)

3. What promises have you made to God and to others? How have you kept them?

Read Judges 14:1–16:4
4. Portray Samson as a young man.

5. What was the nature of Samson's relationship with the Lord?

   Recount each time God is mentioned in these chapters, and what either surprises you or raises questions in your mind.

   What might God be asking of you today that seems unconventional? How can you tell the Lord is in it?

Read Judges 16
6. Characterize Delilah, beginning with her ethnic background.

   How might Delilah have felt about Samson? (See Judges 16:1.)

7. Name Delilah's three motivations for entrapping Samson from Judges 15:20, 16:1, and 16:5 (with Judges 13:3).

8. How might the following passages describe Delilah's tactics?
   Proverbs 1:10, 16:29_____
   Jeremiah 38:22_____
   Acts 20:30_____
   Ephesians 4:14_____

When might you have used similar techniques to your own ends? What was your motivation?

Now, looking back, how might you have done things differently?

9. Twice, Samson divulged a secret, with painful results. Compare:
   <u>Judges 14</u>   <u>Judges 16</u>

10. In view of Samson's upbringing and relationship with God, what might he have told Delilah, when "he told her everything"? (See Judges 16:17.)

    What important truths does it seem Delilah missed?

11. How was Samson undone? (Compare Judges 14:3, 16–17; Judges 16:4, 15–16; James 1:13–15.)

    What patterns do you see in your own life that bring about your "undoing"?

    How can the following Scriptures help you begin to change those patterns?
    Romans 12:1–2_____
    Philippians 1:9–11_____
    Colossians 1:9–12_____
    1 Thessalonians 5:14–22_____

12. What lessons and truths have you learned from studying Delilah's story?

13. What does this passage reveal about God?

14. How is your character and spiritual life challenged by Delilah's story?

15. In what ways will you live out what God is teaching you? Be specific.

INTIMATE

Sinful Woman

Luke 7:36–50

We do not know the sinful woman's backstory at all. A careful reading of her account reveals this is not the same event as when Mary of Bethany anointed Jesus at Simon the Leper's house, and she is also not Mary of Magdala, who had been possessed by seven spirits. (An early conflation, in 581 AD, of stories about these women has since caused much confusion.)

This woman, who had lived a sinful life, was most likely a prostitute: sex trafficking was as common in Jesus' day as it is today, especially among the destitute, impoverished, and desperate. At the very least, she seemed to have had a reputation, for she was immediately recognized, though she remains nameless in this account. Whatever her growing up story, there must have been trauma and soul wounds.

Then she met Jesus.

Again, a careful reading of her whole story will bring pause to Jesus' words concerning her, "her sins, which were many, have been forgiven; hence she has shown great love." (Luke 7:47) At some point she had already come to know Jesus, and even more importantly, Jesus had come to know her, had forgiven her, and restored her.

We know from other parts of the Gospels that Jesus was in the habit of eating with tax collectors and prostitutes—perhaps they had met at such an occasion. Her reputation was now a thing of the past, belonging to the woman she had once been and was no longer. Because of this, her love for

Jesus was so overwhelming the only way she could think to thank him was to pour out her perfume, symbol of her old life's profession, onto his feet.

In ancient times the sort of banquet the Pharisee had provided was often out in the open, like a catered tent wedding might be today. People could stand around and watch the dignitaries and famous celebrities feasting. Outsiders could even hear some of the conversations. Word would go all around town, and often people would go to see who was at the banquet. Like today, it was surely a media event.

It would have been a simple thing for this woman to quietly find Jesus at the banquet table and come up to him. But, because she purposefully took her alabaster jar of perfume with her, it seems reasonable to think she fully intended to anoint Jesus in some way.

Think of all the interactions with people Jesus had had. In all those interactions, Jesus was giving something—giving healing, wisdom, prophecy, warning, instruction, miracles and even food, literally feeding thousands. In how many of those interactions were people giving something to Jesus?

Read Luke 7:36–50

1. From what you know, characterize a Pharisee from Jesus' day.

2. What can you learn about the woman from Luke 7:37–38?

3. Compare the Pharisee to the sinful woman. For example:
   <u>Pharisee</u>   <u>Sinful Woman</u>
   Self-righteous   Sinful

4. In what ways did the Pharisee show respect for Jesus? How did he also show disrespect?

5. In what ways do you honor Jesus? How might you also dishonor him, at times?

6. What did the Pharisee's thought, in Luke 7:39, reveal about his opinion of himself and of Jesus?

   What was Jesus saying about the Pharisee in his parable from Luke 7:41–42?

   Do you think the Pharisee understood what Jesus was saying about him? Why or why not?

7. How would Jesus describe your opinion of him?

8. Contrast the Pharisee's three omissions with the sinful woman's three expressions of love. What meaning might each expression have had?
   Wash feet (Compare with Genesis 18:4, 19:2.)

   Kiss feet (Compare with Genesis 45:15, 1 Samuel 10:1; 20:41.)

   Pour perfume on feet (Compare with Exodus 30:35, Proverbs 27:9.)

9. Jesus told the woman her sins were forgiven. What indicates she may have already heard these words from Jesus? (Compare Luke 7:48 with Luke 7:41–43.)

   Which of your sins do you need to hear Jesus' words over? How will you receive his forgiveness?

10. From the following passages, why was it significant that Jesus would forgive sin?

    Numbers 14:19–20_____

    Numbers 15:28_____

    1 Kings 8:39_____

    2 Chronicles 7:14_____

    Psalm 79:9_____

    Psalm 103:3_____

    Micah 7:18_____

11. What did the sinful woman believe that prompted Jesus' words in Luke 7:50? What do you believe?

12. What lessons and truths have you learned from studying the story of the Sinful Woman?

13. What does this passage reveal about God?

14. How is your character and spiritual life challenged by the Sinful Woman's story?

15. In what ways will you live out what God is teaching you? Be specific.

A FINAL WORD

Acknowledgements

I would not have even conceived of this book without God bringing these biblical women to life through Anita Gutschick and her ministry, Women of the Bible, LLC (womenofthebible.com) and our collaboration in Ancient Voices, Sacred Stories, LLC.

My familiarity with the Scriptures began with a Revised Standard Version of the Bible given to me by the Huguenot Memorial Church of Pelham, New York in 1970. Thank you, Sunday School supervisor, you changed my life.

Becoming involved with Bible Study Fellowship was a turning point in my life. The Bible's stories had already long held me in their thrall, but I learned through BSF how relevant these ancient words are to me personally and to the world around me. Through my years of studying, teaching, and writing with BSF, I have come to appreciate the importance and value of a truly in-depth study in which three important steps are acknowledged: What does the text say? What does the text mean? How will I live out these truths in my every day?

I hold out special gratitude to Bonnie Zadoretzky, my close friend, teacher, and mentor for many years; Karen Crout, faithful coworker and prayer partner; and Cindy Hunter, sensitive and perceptive storyteller. These three heart friends and wise women in the Lord have listened to countless hours of my thoughts and ideas and always steered me well.

Dr. Bill Clark taught me how to understand the inside of a person, especially the inside of me, and by extension, the insides of the people whose stories are recorded in Scripture.

Julie Zine Coleman, published author and speaker, emboldened me to start writing.

Natasha, Mari, and Julia, my beloved daughters, literally healed me just by being part of my life. I am who I am today because they drew me back from the brink. I admire who they are becoming in their own worlds and am so thankful for their support, reading my stuff, and helping me put to words all these visions in my head. Through their eyes I took a fresh look at the women within these Scriptures who will be their companions long after I have joined the ancients in heaven.

David, my most beloved companion and partner in life, fellow creator and best editor I could have ever hoped for or imagined, has made me write far better than I ever would have without his patient and astute observations. His wisdom, brilliance, empathy, and intelligence exhort me, encourage me, spur me on, and keep the wind under my wings.

Meet the Author

Joanne Guarnieri Hagemeyer

When she received her own Bible at the age of nine, she read the whole book, from preface to concordance, with transcendent joy, knowing these were the very words of God. Today, Joanne continues in God's call to teach, counsel, mentor, and train in his word and Spirit through retreats, Bible studies, and online classes.

After leading and teaching a Bible class of 350–500 students from 2003 to 2013, then retiring in 2018 as an advisor and mentor to eight Bible classes in the Maryland area through Bible study Fellowship, Joanne began teaching and speaking through Ancient Voices, Sacred Stories, LLC, and with Grace and Peace. She also serves on the pulpit teaching team of her church, New Hope Chapel, Arnold, MD.

A long-time "armchair archaeologist," Joanne joined the Board of Directors for the Biblical Archaeology Forum in 2013 and has participated in two excavations, Tel Kabri and Tel Akko, Israel. She also serves as a counselor and trainer in affiliation with Lay Counselor Institute since 2012. Joanne is currently attending Portland Seminary, working towards a Master's in Theological Studies.

www.ingramcontent.com/pod-product-compliance
Lightning Source LLC
Chambersburg PA
CBHW071439160426
43195CB00013B/1969